Tom,

Here's to
& single malt scotch
for days!

← Haiku!

The Fried Twinkie Manifesto

and other tales of disaster and damnation

The Fried Twinkie Manifesto

and other tales of disaster and damnation

Ryan Moehring

Author's note: Most of the stories in this book are inspired by real events. Some are embellished. Others are completely fabricated. Characters based on real people have fictitious names and identifying features. If you happen to see your name anywhere in the text, then you probably have a pretty common name. Either way, if we've never met, please assume that the story in question isn't about you. I must mention that neither the Hostess® brand nor Twinkies® have any affiliation whatsoever with this poor excuse for literature. In fact, I'm confident they wouldn't approve of it at all.

Special thanks are due to the following gentlemen, who gracefully endured my bouts of premature manopause as we pieced this book together.

Editing and Typesetting: Ben Dayton

Cover Design: Jacob Custer

Interior Illustrations: Jared Moehring (my very funny fourteen-year-old brother)

For my Faceless Wonder

Contents

The Fried Twinkie Manifesto

and other tales of disaster and damnation

The Devil Knows Best

The Mexican word for drinking straw is *popote.* I learned this while finishing my bachelor's degree in Mexico. What I didn't know at the time was nearly every Latin American country has its own word for straw, and when you order a *piña colada con un popote* in, let's say, Nicaragua (or virtually any other Latin American country), you're asking for a piña colada with a side order of poop. *Popo* means poop, which makes *popote* a big pile of poop. I must have ordered poop with my mixed drinks in three different countries before one kind bartender alerted me to the error of my ways.

Besides naming their straws after piles of excrement, I also learned that Mexicans eat nearly every meal together as a family. After lunch and dinner, they have a *sobremesa,* during which

everyone sits around talking, drinking coffee, and smoking cigarettes. I enjoyed the tradition because it allowed me to get to know
my Mexican host family and my two gringo roommates. But more
importantly, it provided me with an opportunity to practice my
Spanish, which I desperately needed. My Spanish sounded something like a Special Olympics gold-medal winner with a speech
impediment struggling through his acceptance speech—while
tripping on psychedelic mushrooms.

At the end of the first week of the semester, my roommates and
I attended a school-sponsored retreat to a nearby natural spring.
When we returned, I recounted the story of the excursion to my
host family during an after-lunch *sobremesa.* I told them that on
the way home, a group of girls sat with us in the back of the bus,
flirting with us the whole time. As Maria, my surrogate *Mamá*,
gasped in horror, I instantly knew I had said something wrong.
I later learned that I had confused the word for flirting, *coquetear*,
with *chaquetear*, which means to jack off. It took Maria's husband,
Guillermo, a week to convince her that I wasn't a sexual deviant
who needed to be locked in his room at night.

Everyone called Guillermo "Memo," for short. He was a
serious-looking man in his early sixties, with a tight bottom lip
and very handsome features. He fancied himself a gentleman and
took great pleasure in showing off his extensive art collection to
anyone who would indulge him. If you liked a particular painting or sculpture, Memo would provide you with a detailed story
about the inspiration behind the piece, as well as point out those
works containing personalized tributes by his artist friends.

I spoke the best Spanish of the three American students living under Memo's roof, and apparently had the best grasp on art history. I mercifully restrained myself whenever a tribute on a painting or piece of pottery was made out to someone else other than Memo, or when a painting he claimed was given to him by a close friend and famous Mexican artist was actually a drug-store print by Rembrandt or Picasso. He declined to comment when I asked him how long he and Monet had been friends.

Art defined Memo. He had spent his whole life working for the local phone company, and even now, as a senior citizen, he was regularly asked to make the long drive from *Cuernavaca* over the mountain pass into Mexico City to help with particularly complex issues. The only material possessions he had to show for his lifetime of work were his art collection and his house, which fittingly, was situated on *Calle del Artista*—Artist Street. Memo proudly told me one afternoon that the street was named after Paul Newman, who lived in this exact house in the late sixties when he and Robert Redford filmed *Butch Cassidy & the Sundance Kid*. According to Memo, my room was the exact same in which the famous American icon had stayed during filming.

Memo's eldest son had slept in that bedroom after Paul, and now it was my turn to enjoy the view that overlooked the back-yard garden and pool. Some nights I would pop out the screen of my window, smoke a joint, close my eyes, and replay famous scenes from the movie. My favorite scene to reenact was Butch (played by me) and the Sundance Kid holding up a Bolivian bank with a crib sheet and our pistols, neither of us able to communicate well enough in Spanish to get the message across to the bank teller. *"Dame todo el money before I shoot you in the stinking cabeza,*

3

cucaracha!"

Maybe it was the fact that Memo saw a bit of Paul Newman in me, or perhaps it was because I was the only one whose Spanish was good enough to have a semi-normal conversation with him—whatever it was, he took a liking to me. While my somewhat younger roommates were out on the town stalking women, Memo and I would stay up late, making *mojitos* with the fresh mint from his garden and arguing about any number of topics. Religion, politics, sex; no subject was off-limits, and more often than not, Memo and I found ourselves on opposite sides of the fence. After seven or eight drinks one night, I told him that instead of going with my roommates to Acapulco the following weekend, I intended to travel three hours to the Aztec ruins at *Teotihuacán*. As a man who appreciated art and culture, his reaction surprised me.

"Why do you want to travel all day long to look at the crumbling pyramids of a failed, blood-thirsty civilization?" He harshly slurred in Spanish. "Besides, these days it is nothing more than a dusty tourist trap."

I gave him my standard academic response. "Because Aztec origins are a vital part of what it means to be a modern Mexican. Octavio Paz once said that Mexicans are not only enigmatic to others, but also to themselves. Maybe if Mexicans were more in touch with their heritage, they wouldn't be—"

"Ay, puta madre," Memo interjected with a dismissive wave of his hand. "This! This is exactly my point. You read too many books. You don't *live* enough. You see this?" He gestured toward one of the several nude female portraits hanging in his mini art gallery. "This is what you need, Ryan. You are young. Go with

4

your friends to Acapulco and get laid. Get some pussy while you still can. Before you know it, you will be married with kids and working a job that you hate. Your woman will get fat. Then what? Life will be over for you, my friend."

I shook my head, speechless.

"Trust me, *mi'jo*. I know what I'm talking about. *Más sabe el Diablo por viejo que por Diablo*." He then stood up on his wobbly legs and braced himself against the table before leaving. "I have to piss."

With that, Memo left the room. I waited for nearly twenty minutes, staring at the nude artwork on the wall and finishing the last of my drink, but he did not return. I lay awake in Paul Newman's bedroom that night, thinking about what Memo had said about the Devil. The saying roughly translates to "The Devil knows more from being old than from being the Devil." An equivalent proverb might be "With age comes wisdom," or as Julius Caesar once said, "Experience is the greatest teacher."

Before I fell asleep that night, I pulled out my copy of the complete works of Tomás Rivera, one of the most well-known Chicano authors. The author's parents were migrant workers of Mexican descent, and his stories center on his childhood experiences growing up on farms across America. Like Memo, Rivera's parents were devout Catholics, and despite their unrelenting hardships, they were steadfast in their faith. Young Rivera resents their superstitions, because, as he sees it, if God really existed, he would not allow the Devil to cause them so much suffering. After all, they said their prayers every night and went to mass every week. They were good people, but for some reason, God continued to allow the Devil to punish them. One night, despite his uncle's warning, he decides to take matters into his own hands. Young Rivera sneaks outside, exactly at midnight, and tries to confront the Devil himself.

Unsure what to call him, he tries all the names he knows: "Devil! Lucifer! Satan!" But he receives no reply. Next, he thinks it might be better to curse the Devil. He uses every cuss word he has ever heard—he even curses the Devil's mother, but still nothing happens. It is just him, all alone, in the peaceful, silvery night. Emboldened by this apparent victory, he declares that there is no Devil. But if there is no Devil, then neither is there a—but he doesn't dare finish the sentence.

In Rivera's stories, the youth are portrayed as heroes who transcend the ignorance and superstitions of their elders. Reading that story reminded me of my discussion with Memo that night. *The Devil isn't smart because he's old,* I thought. *The Devil doesn't even exist.* I liked Memo, but he was just wrong about the ruins. I'd take ancient pyramids over getting laid any day.

The weekend came, and Memo still had not talked me out of going to the ruins. Convinced that trying to change my mind was a lost cause, he instead focused on making sure I knew exactly where to go and what to say to the people I encountered on my journey. He volunteered to give me a ride to the bus stop, mostly I think, so he could quiz me. "What is the name of the subway stop that will take you to your second bus?"

"We've already gone over this, Memo. *Indio Verde.*"

"Perhaps if you would stop smoking all of those goddamned marijuana cigarettes you could remember something for once in your pitiful life. It's *Indios Verdes.* Plural. They still teach plural in those godforsaken American schools of yours, no?"

I looked at him in disbelief. "Yes, *mi'jo*," he said. "I know all about your little stash of marijuana. You can't bring any with you to the pyramids, by the way. So, if you have some with you, you need to give it to me now."

Fortuitously, the very first person I met when I arrived at Mexico City's airport was a drug dealer named Freddy. When Freddy picked me up in his car to sell me pot, he asked me how much I wanted. "I don't know," I said. "How much will forty bucks get me?"

It turns out that forty dollars gets you a lot—certainly more than I wanted or needed, and enough, were I to get caught carrying it, to land me in a Mexican prison for a very long time. My roommates and I spent the first two days rolling enough joints to last us the whole summer. Our hands got tired after number one hundred and seventy-seven, so we decided that would have to last us for a while. The rest we divided up into smaller bags and sold to other students to pay for our excursions and nights out on the town.

"But Memo, I always wanted to get high on top of a pyramid," I protested.

"And I always wanted to fuck four women at the same time. You can't always get what you want. That's The Rolling Stones. You should know this."

"I hate the Rolling Stones."

"Goddamned Americans," he retorted. "Screw up the entire planet and don't even appreciate the few things you actually contribute to the world."

"The Rolling Stones are British, genius." It wasn't very often that I was able to prove Memo wrong, so I relished every opportunity.

He quietly cursed me in Spanish.

When we arrived at the bus station, I reluctantly handed Memo the joint I had stashed in my bag. I got out of the car and asked him to take my picture. *"Me la sacas, Memo?"* Several bystanders turned their heads and gave me dirty looks.

Memo frowned. "God help us," he muttered.

In Spanish, if you forget to say one word it can completely change the meaning of the entire sentence. I later learned that instead of saying, "Will you take my picture?" I said something closer to, "Will you pull it out for me?"

As I started toward the bus station, Memo called me back to the car. "Listen, boy," he whispered. "This is not like the *Estados Unidos* where you can just go anywhere and do anything you like. The police are corrupt and they will try to get you into trouble if they can. If you have any problems, do not argue with them. Just give them this and they will leave you alone." He slipped a $20 bill in my hand and closed the car door. As I tried to protest he pointed to his temple with a boyish grin and said, *"Más sabe el Diablo,* Ryan." He turned the key, revved the engine, and drove away.

By the time I arrived at the ruins I was gushing with excitement. I read in one of my books during the bus ride that the base of the Pyramid of the Sun was larger than the Great Pyramid in Egypt. *This is going to be an epic adventure,* I thought. However, when

I got off the bus my enthusiasm quickly deflated. On both sides of the quarter-mile-long road that led to the ruins' entrance were at least one hundred vendors selling the same, cheaply-constructed NAFTA-era souvenirs you find on street corners in every part of Mexico. Some of the booths were occupied by children no older than nine or ten. These vendors clearly lived in the vast slum that surrounded the ruins, and were likely being exploited by some Mexico-City-based manufacturer. I wondered if somewhere in those slums was a boy, not unlike Rivera, who someday would sneak out under the twilight and boldly curse the Devil.

The complex at Teotihuacán is indescribable. A brochure I picked up on my walk toward the ruins claimed that the site covered more than 80 square kilometers and that at its height, around 450 A.D., the city was home to nearly 200,000 inhabitants. Since the majority of the historically-relevant monuments were located along the Avenue of the Dead, I decided to go there first and check out the huge pyramids at either end of the road.

In ancient times they called Teotihuacán, "the place where men go to become gods." I found out very quickly that today it is nothing more than a bustling tourist trap where vendors and tourists alike come to be exploited.

"Excuse me, sir," a teenage local said to me in impeccable English. "Allow me to introduce myself. My name is Manuel Angél Gutierrez de la Rosa. I am a citizen of Teotihuacán, and I would be honored if you would allow me to be your tour guide today and show you all of the magnificent splendors of this archeological treasure."

"Thank you, Manuel, but I need not services of guiding temples this same day," I responded in my infantile Spanish. His look was one of confusion that faded into disappointment. "But the most good of luck for you," I added. "It appears as though there are many sweaty people here who would love to pay you for showing them how to make love to these old rocks." He walked away without a word.

Months later, after my Spanish had improved tremendously, I often used this tactic to ward-off pesky vendors. Two of my favorite phrases were: "My explosive diarrhea is angry at your face," and "The benevolent herpes monster that lives inside the castle in my pants would like to cross your moat."

I walked through the crowd, trying my best to admire the architecture of the ruins, but with all of the tourists around, distractions were inescapable. Perhaps the loudest of these disturbances was a small American child, no older than nine, who was throwing a temper tantrum in the middle of the main plaza. "But mommy, I WANT that baby doll NOW! Pleeeeeeease, mommy! I'll be good—please just buy me the baby!"

"Now, sweetheart, we've already gone over this," her mother rationalized. "If you're a good girl we might consider buying you the baby later, ok, angel? You know, when you scream like that it hurts mommy's feelings. You don't want to hurt your mommy's feelings, do you?"

"I hate you, mommy! You're the worst mommy in the whole world! I hope you fall down the pyramid and die! Waaaaaaaaaah!"

"Well, mommy loves you anyway, my little angel."

This was not at all what I had anticipated, so I decided to climb to the top of the main pyramid, thinking its heights might provide me some refuge from screaming toddlers. Before I reached the base of the pyramid, a man handed me a flier. Apparently Walmart had purchased land directly adjacent to the ancient city, and was planning on building a giant superstore to "serve" the surrounding population. The flier stated that the building site contained precious artifacts, and since *Teotihuacán* was a UNESCO World Heritage Site, it was illegal to build upon it. I stuffed the piece of paper into my pocket and shook my head. Memo was right about everything. I began my ascent.

The Pyramid of the Sun has exactly three hundred and sixty-five steps, one for each day of the year. Most of the steps have had their edges worn down by the footsteps of millions of visitors over thousands of years, making their navigation a bit tricky. Once on top, I sat down on the sacrificial alter and admired the view. To my right was the Pyramid of the Moon, and behind it, the Sierra Madre Oriental mountain range stretched out into the distance.

The summit of the pyramid was surprisingly high, and the people walking around down below looked like busy ants at work. I was thankful that I couldn't hear any of them or their screaming children. For a moment I resented Memo for taking my joint, because this was the perfect place to get high, but then I thought back to his reaction when I told him of my intentions to come here.

He had been right about this place. The obnoxious tourists, the screaming children, the exploitation of the vendors—it was all too much. And now the multinationals were coming with their bulldozers.

The negativity was beginning to overwhelm me, when off in the dusty, cactus-laden distance I saw a bus approaching the complex. I suddenly wanted out of this place, and the next bus to Mexico City wasn't coming for another two hours. If I was going to catch that bus I needed to hurry. I sprinted down the sheer steps, nearly plummeting to my death several times like the countless human sacrifices before me. As I made my descent, I imagined Aztec parents taking their kids to watch the sacrifices: "Mommy, mommy, when are they going to rip out the heart?"

"Shh, child. Very soon. We must be patient."

"But, mommy, I want to see them rip out the heart nooooooow!"

When I reached the bottom I took a deep breath, dusted myself off, and raced to the bus loading area. On the way out of the complex, I noticed the same little girl's parents buying her the doll she so coveted. As I passed through the vendors' square, the sweet aroma of roasted pork filled my nostrils. I heard a man yell something in Spanish that sounded like, "Stop, chorizo!" but as tempting as a chorizo sausage snack was, I needed to catch that bus. I ignored my hunger pangs and continued sprinting. I reached the loading area with just enough time to catch my breath while I waited for the last handful of passengers to board.

This was a state bus, so it would be packed with locals and the fare would be cheap. I looked around as I paid the driver twenty pesos, noticing that I was the only gringo on board. I made my way to the back of the bus and sat down in front of a young man who was playing "Hotel California" on his acoustic guitar. The bus took off and I reclined in my seat, relaxing to the guitar's melody.

Twenty minutes into the trip, I had almost fallen asleep when the hydraulic brakes screeched and the bus came to a stop. Two men dressed completely in black boarded the bus—M16 assault rifles in hand—and surveyed the faces of the passengers. If these chaps got on your bus in America you could be certain that something was terribly wrong, but Memo had warned me about the Mexican Federal police and their overly-dramatic tactics, so I didn't panic. I heard one of them say *gringo*, and I sighed heavily as they walked towards me. *Naturally,* I thought. *In the middle of the Mexican desert, two angry men with assault rifles are looking for me.*

One of the men asked me in Spanish to open my backpack, saying something about *chorizo*. "A thousand sorries, sir," I cordially replied in his language. "What business has you with my gigantic sausage? Everybody in this places seems to be in love with my sausage, yes?"

"Open the backpack," he repeated in Spanish, confused by my response, but undaunted.

"Listen, dude," I responded in English. "If this is some kind of joke, it's not funny. I know that sausage guy is probably pretty broke, and on most days I would have bought lunch from him, but I was in a hurry, OK?"

"Open the backpack."

"Is that the only sentence you know?" I started in English. "You might be the only person in Mexico whose Spanish is worse than mine." I tried to continue in Spanish, "I knows not what you think in your fat Latin brain, but I read on occasions about the

13

constitution of Mexico's greatest nation, and even foreign intrud-
ing viruses such as me is protected from the searching, even so far
up as seizures in the anal cavity. Now you understands me, yes? I
have no sausage in my sack."

The man paused for a second, clearly confounded by what
had just escaped from my mouth, and trying to decide if he should
be offended. "Open the backpack, *chorizo*," he said, emphasizing
the last word as if it were an insult. Why this guy had nick-named
me after a spicy sausage I did not know, but he was persistent. He
was also now pointing his gun directly at my face.

"Jesus Christ. All this over some goddamn sausage?" I had
given up speaking Spanish to them. It was going to be all English
from this point on. "Memo was right—you guys are a bunch of
lunatics. Fine, have it your way." I handed the backpack to him.
"What happens next, are you going to plant some chorizo in my
backpack and take me down to the precinct?"

All I had in my backpack was my passport, my wallet, a
couple of liters of water, the Tomás Rivera book, a bottle of sun-
screen, three granola bars, and a digital camera. The twenty-dollar
bill Memo had given me, along with the rest of my money, was
stashed safely in my sock. It didn't take long before the police
officer realized that I did not, in fact, have any stolen sausage in
my backpack, and that my passport matched the only wallet in
my possession. He threw my bag back at me and departed with a
grunt. Before I knew it, the bus was moving again. I noticed several
of the passengers staring at me, which made me uncomfortable. I
shrugged at a woman across the aisle and said, "I don't even like
chorizo that much." She glared at me accusingly, as if I were some

sort of perverted sausage addict.

I asked the man with the guitar sitting behind me if he would let me play his instrument for a while, but he just gave me a dirty look and silently stared out the window for the remainder of the ride. I've had the good fortune of being punched in the face many times over the years, and I could tell from those experiences that this guy had a sincere hankering for punching me square in my nose. *Mexicans, especially Mexican men, are very proud,* I thought. *Maybe it's an insult to ask to play another man's guitar?*

Memo was waiting for me at the bus stop. When I got in the car he grinned and said, "I bet you wish you had gone to Acapulco and gotten laid, yes?" The look on my face apparently said it all, and he laughed, relishing his victory. I tossed my bag in the back of the car, and as we drove away I recounted the events of the day to him. When I told him about the incident with the police on the bus he laughed so hard that I thought he might crash the car. "You actually believed that they thought you were a sausage thief?! Hahahaha! A *chorizo* is a pick pocket, you moron—they thought you had stolen someone's wallet! God has sent me this shit-for-brains for amusement!"

I then asked him about the guitar player and why he had acted so strange when I asked to play his guitar. "You asked him what? Oh my god, just when I thought it could not get any funnier, you top even yourself! *Eres pendejo, o nomás te haces?* You know that you asked this man if you could touch his penis? You are lucky he did not punch you right in your stupid American face. If you value your life you do not say such things to a Mexican man. Oh my god, the comedy! What have I done to be so blessed today?"

"Yeah, yeah," I responded, blushing. "Laugh all you want, old man. But seriously, I guess I need to thank you. After all, if you hadn't made me give you that joint, you'd be bailing me out of jail instead of picking me up from the bus station."

"This is true, Ryan. And you know why? It's because the Devil is smarter from being old than from being the Devil. If your empty head remembers nothing else that I have said to you, remember this."

Memo fumbled through his ash tray and pulled out the joint he had taken from me earlier. He lit it, took a couple of puffs, and broke the silence before I could express my shock. *Memo smokes pot?*

"You know, Ryan," he said with a strained voice while holding in a lungful of smoke, "You should not feel so bad about making these mistakes with your Spanish." He took several more puffs and passed it to me. "Even big companies do this sometimes. I remember an airline commercial many years ago. They were trying to advertise their new leather seats and extra leg room in first class. The problem was that their slogan, 'fly in leather,' sounded like 'fly naked' when translated into Spanish. Get it? Those sonsabitches were saying that when you flew naked with them they would give you three extra inches. Hahahaha!"

Before long, we took the final puffs of the joint and our laughter died. We were quiet as Memo drove the car over the mountain pass, revealing the beautiful valley below. A brilliant red-orange sun was beginning to set over the ridge in the west, bathing the valley in a rich, scarlet hue. Memo and I weren't exactly Butch Cassidy and the Sundance Kid, but we were friends, and I felt for a moment that we were riding off into the sunset in an old western movie. The devil was nowhere in sight.

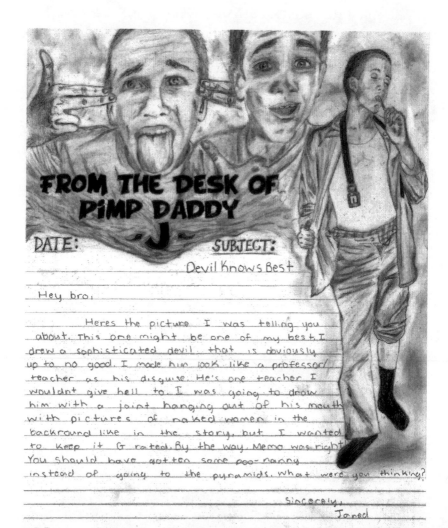

FROM THE DESK OF PIMP DADDY
-J-

DATE: _____   SUBJECT:
                                   Devil Knows Best

Hey bro,

     Heres the picture I was telling you about. This one might be one of my best I drew a sophisticated devil that is obviously up to no good. I made him look like a professor/ teacher as his disguise. He's one teacher I wouldn't give hell to. I was going to draw him with a joint hanging out of his mouth with pictures of naked women in the backround like in the story, but I wanted to keep it G rated. By the way, Memo was right. You should have gotten some poo-nanny instead of going to the pyramids. What were you thinking?

                    Sincerely,
                    Jared

Betting on Heaven

From the time I was a small child and into my adult years, my born-again Christian family—and countless other well-intentioned friends and acquaintances—cited Pascal's wager as a reason why I should believe in God. The essence of Blaise Pascal's famous wager is simple: Choose to believe in God, and if you're wrong you lose nothing. Your corpse rots in the earth, and you become worm food just like everything else. But if you believe in God and you're right, you gain everything. You go to Heaven and enjoy every conceivable pleasure, courtesy of the Host of Hosts. However, if you bet against God and you're wrong, you lose everything. You burn in a fiery hell for all of eternity. The kicker is you have no choice—you have to bet.

Even at nine-years-old I realized that these people didn't

want me to believe in just any god. They had plenty of words to describe the wacky beliefs of those who held different religious points of view than them. "Goddamn Jews," they would say in their self-righteous certainty. "They're going to burn in Hell with those fucking Mormons." I would be the first person to concede that the Mormons were a weird bunch of "bike guys with ties," as I called them as a kid, though I wouldn't go so far as to speculate about their eternal damnation.

My grandfather converted to Mormonism for a short time when I was young, and as a result of my many interactions with Mormons, I know more than I ever wanted to know about their religion. My grandpa didn't buy into their beliefs, and I'm fairly sure he believed they were all going to Hell, but the Church of Jesus Christ of Latter Day Saints helped new converts pay their medical bills, and that's all the convincing my business-savvy grandpa needed during one family crisis. I can only imagine that he thought it was his spiritual duty to relieve these "cult" members of their money.

During the conversion process, Mormon bike riders would regularly descend upon my grandparents' house on their Huffy and Schwinn steeds to share their gospel with us. I soon learned that they believed in what, to me, were some truly absurd things. For example, they wore special diaper-looking undergarments that they believed would help preserve their chastity. According to Joseph Smith, the founder and "prophet" of Mormonism, God's throne was situated near a star called Kolob, where time was measured at one-thousand human years to one Kolob day. They also preached that Heaven had multiple levels, and they actually had some pretty convincing maps to support their claims. You couldn't ascend to the highest circle of Heaven (presumably where all the beer-pong parties and orgies took place) unless you gave the church ten percent of your income. A heavenly VIP lounge, if you will.

These beliefs, I admit, are strange. However, my Christian family had some bizarre ideas of their own. First of all, they believed with every fiber of their beings that the earth was no more than ten-thousand-years-old. When staring up at a twenty-foot Tyrannosaurus Rex skeleton they might tell you that the fossils—that *all* fossils for that matter—were fake. The skeletons were clearly part of some secular plot to disprove God's existence. But they couldn't tell you exactly how the bones were created, nor how they were buried beneath hundreds of feet of impermeable rock. It was the Cold War, and it was easy to blame the conspiracy on the godless Communists in Russia. The Russians had the ability to infiltrate the CIA and to create nuclear weapons capable of obliterating all life as we knew it, so by comparison, the small matter of fabricating phony dinosaur bones was child's play.

My family also believed that unseen forces were constantly waging war for the possession of our souls. Every one of us had an invisible guardian angel whose job was to protect us from Satan's legion of demons. Apparently these guardian angels were hopelessly outnumbered, because their defenses were frequently penetrated by the demonic forces. Instead of attributing Cousin Johnny's case of crabs to his proclivity to hookers or Uncle Dave's alcoholism to his unhappy marriage, my family would blame Satan's henchmen.

On occasions when our heavenly protections broke down, the most overzealous of my relatives would hold emergency prayer sessions to cast out the malevolent spirits. Scripture told my family that whenever two or more believers called upon the Lord, he would fill them with the Holy Spirit, which would then aid them in whatever it was they were trying to accomplish. You knew a person had invoked the Holy Spirit when they spoke in tongues.

For the uninitiated, this is basically a silly, made-up language some Christians convince themselves they can speak when under the influence of the Holy Spirit. Once you get past the creepiness of the concept, it's actually quite entertaining to watch. For example, "Satan, I command you to remove your crabs from Johnny's pubic hair," might sound like, "Hashannala mooby williwa nee-how ichiban Nasho tarleenger-lee."

The ritual sounded to me like a bunch of mentally challenged Chinese hillbillies fighting over the last pot sticker. But if I wanted to take a magic spaceship ride in my special underwear to pray to the Mormon god on planet Kolob, that would somehow be stranger to my family than talking in a made-up, incomprehensible language to cast out the demonic spirit of venereal diseases.

No, they wanted me to believe in their god, which I didn't. Perhaps the best word is: couldn't. Have you ever tried believing in something you didn't? Impossible. It's like trying to convince yourself that smoking copious amounts of marijuana is a spiritual catalyst—that it might allow you secret insights into the inner workings of the universe. Despite what the Hippies may tell you, it just doesn't work. Trust me, I've tried it. The only divine insight I ever received while stoned was that mint chocolate chip ice cream pairs beautifully with Funyuns.

For most kids, there wouldn't be much debate about Pascal's wager. "That sounds like a great deal, mom," an ordinary child might say. "God is real, and I can't wait to go meet him in Heaven. Can I go play now?" But I wasn't like most kids. I was exceptionally inquisitive. I asked my parents so many questions about God that to this day they regret ever mentioning him or his heaven to me at all. Especially my poor dad, who it seemed to me, couldn't have cared less about the subject. But for fear of retribution from my mother and her evangelical family, he didn't dare question a word of it.

I wondered if you had to go to school in Heaven, or eat vegetables. "Does Heaven have a sun and a moon?" I would ask. "What about day and night? Do you sleep there? Do they have a special squadron of angels who punish you for sanctioning a cage fight between your sister's hamster and your best friend's ferret?" These questions invariably crinkled the foreheads of the adults in my family, but failed to elicit concrete answers.

For people who spoke so authoritatively about God, it seemed to me that they didn't know very much about him or his afterlife. I wanted details. "What time is dinner?" I asked. "What do you *mean* you don't know if they eat? Will I still be a kid when I go there, or can I be an adult? Do they have school in Heaven? What about recess? Monkey bars? *Please* tell me they're going to have monkey bars. Will my best friend Nick be there? What do you *mean* you're not sure? What does God have against Mexicans?"

Then one day my great-grandfather died. I saw people cry

so hard that I thought they might die themselves, right there in the funeral parlor. I remember realizing that my great-grandfather was a Christian, which meant that while his family was mourning his death, he was probably shooting four-under on the back nine of the most beautiful golf course this side of the Andromeda galaxy. Heaven was supposedly the best place you could go, so I wondered why they weren't celebrating for him. They clearly weren't mourning because they liked him, or were going to miss him very much. After Alzheimer's set in, he spent most of his time sitting in a chair in my grandparents' living room, watching The People's Court and pooping his pants.

Not exactly the life of the party.

I suppose they were crying because they were scared. It's very easy to profess your belief in an afterlife when singing hymnals in the comfort of a church pew. But when you're staring at the cold, lifeless heap of a relative, who just days before was merrily whistling the Andy Griffith theme song while pissing on an antique rug, mortality's icy embrace sends shivers down the spine of even the most faithful. Compound an inherently frightening subject with a cast of born-again authority figures who were all-too-eager to share their stories of demonic visions with me, and obsessing about the afterlife became my nightly bedtime ritual.

I remember praying, *Now I lay me down to sleep, I pray to Lord my soul to keep. If I die before I wake, I pray the Lord my soul to take.* But I didn't really understand, let alone mean, the words I spoke. I honestly didn't know what my soul was, but even as a small boy I had a hunch that it was important, and I wanted to hang on to it. The proposition of my soul being taken from me while I slept, by some scary, bearded guy in the sky (who I had never personally met, and who apparently had a track record of sentencing people to eternal damnation) just didn't sit well. I liked my soul, whatever it was, and I wanted to keep it.

Besides, why was everyone so preoccupied with the afterlife anyway? Why couldn't they just enjoy this life? Growing up in the vast open spaces of the Rocky Mountains was wonderful. I could play all day in the beautiful mountain valley near our home without any grown-ups around telling me what to do. I couldn't imagine Heaven being any better, especially with it full of adults who spoke in their own invented languages. How could anyone understand each other?

One summer day when I was nine, I was skateboarding outside with my friends when I saw my favorite aunt's car pull into our driveway. I rushed home to see her. When I entered the house she was already engaged in a religious conversation with my mother. As I rummaged for a chocolate fix in the pantry, I overheard my aunt mention a term I had never heard before: born again.

"What does that mean?" I interrupted. Like Nicodemus two thousand years before me, I wondered if being born again meant that you had to go back inside your mom and pop out again. The mere thought sent shivers down my spine. Even if my everlasting salvation was at stake, there was no way that was going to happen.

Not back inside *her*.

Perhaps the only one in my family who had actually read the Bible and could quote John 3:3, my aunt went on to tell me that you cannot go to Heaven until you are born again, which she interpreted as "accepting Jesus Christ into your heart." She told me that we all had sin inside of us, which was a bad thing. We needed to invite Jesus inside our hearts so that he could cleanse us of that sin. Then we could all go to Heaven and be happy.

That sounded pretty easy to me, and I wondered why everybody didn't do it. But the more I learned about Christianity in Sunday school, the less sense it made to me. As I understood it, God floated around by himself for gazillions of years in the middle of outer space, presumably playing the world's longest game of Solitaire or Go Fish to pass the time. Understandably, after countless years of asking himself to "go fish," he got lonely and decided to create other living things to keep himself company. I was an only child, so I could empathize with his loneliness. What I couldn't understand was how, after having a kajillion years to plan an ideal world, a perfect god would consciously choose to create a planet as completely and utterly screwed up as ours.

The Garden of Eden fable ultimately convinced me that Jehovah, if he even existed at all, was imperfect. After celebrating his so-called "best creations," God commanded them not to eat the forbidden fruit. But he then created the much more intelligent Devil, fully aware of the fact that Satan would trick them—free will or not—into doing exactly what he had just forbidden. When Adam and Eve inevitably fell into this carefully-laid trap, God punished them by permanently banishing them from paradise.

Even the State of California and Major League Baseball offer a three strike policy, but not God. Instead of just giving them a second chance like any of his compassionate, albeit flawed creations would do, God cast them out of paradise and cursed their future offspring with original sin. Then, just I was beginning to think that God couldn't possibly seem any more irrational, he devised the ingenious plan of sacrificing his only son to cancel out Adam and Eve's sins—the same sins he specifically designed them to commit in the first place, and sins he could have forgiven with a wave of his hand. Jesus supposedly endured a horrible, agonizing death over a simple piece of fruit, and as a result, any hypocritical, hateful person could get into Heaven just by swearing a few simple words of allegiance to him. Even as a kid, God sounded to me like an irrational, contemptible bully.

Who kills their son anyway?

Since the story seemed so ridiculous to me, I began to wonder if God was like Santa Claus and the Tooth Fairy. I wondered if he was just one of those made-up stories parents told their kids to get them to behave. I found a bag of my teeth in my mom's top dresser drawer a week before my seventh birthday, and after a little prodding, she confessed the fairy tale. Just months after that discovery, my friend Nick and I stayed up late on Christmas Eve and caught his dad eating the cookies we had left out for Santa. Who could say for certain that adults weren't lying about God too?

God had to be a phony, at least their god. Of that much I was pretty sure. None of my family had ever really talked to God— they just read the Bible and went to church. Everything they knew about God they had learned from somebody else. I tried to talk to God and Jesus every single day for years, but they never talked back.

Why would God ignore a little kid?

The fact that nobody else acknowledged what I could see so clearly left me feeling isolated. I didn't believe in Jesus, so I couldn't accept him into my heart. According to their religious beliefs, that meant I was going to Hell. When you're nine-years-old and your family believes you're going to burn in a fiery pit of misery for all-time while they drink frozen daiquiris in paradise, words cannot describe the loneliness you feel.

These feelings of isolation festered inside of me for the next decade, and eventually turned into bitterness. During my eighteenth birthday party, I revealed to my family that I had become an orthodox minister. They were elated to hear the news, and I allowed them nearly thirty seconds of congratulations before delivering the punch line. "Five-minute online application—Hallelujah!—Father Ryan's in the house, bitches!"

I didn't delay putting my new-found credentials to use, crashing family Bible studies with examples of unexplained inconsistencies and strange scriptures I had encountered in their holy book.

"If Proverbs 12:21 says that 'no evil shall happen to the just,' then why did God allow Job, a humble servant of the Lord, to be tortured by Satan?"

"In II Kings, God commands two bears to maul forty-two children as punishment for mocking Elisha. What happened to an eye for an eye?"

"If God is perfect, then how could he be jealous, as he proclaims in Exodus? Isn't jealousy a human emotion, and a flaw?"

"Deuteronomy says that no man whose testicles are crushed, or whose penis is cut off may enter the Kingdom of Heaven. Were evil men commonly subjected to nut crushing in those days, or are crushed testicles simply another of God's pet peeves?"

"Why does God condone slavery in the book of Deuteronomy when even young children know slavery to be wrong?"

"Why, oh why does God tell Ezekiel in chapter four, verse twelve, to cook bread with his own poop? Somebody? Anybody?"

Again, I received the same crinkled foreheads and uncomfortable looks as when I was a child, but no satisfactory responses. "There are some things that we're just not supposed to understand, Ryan," was the standard response. "It's all in God's hands." What bothered me most was the fact that, despite their supposed salvation, no one in my family seemed to be happy, or to even strive for happiness. They had resigned themselves to their fate. A lifetime of blind obedience was a small price to pay for an eternity of bliss, and they dutifully accepted their sacrifice. Though they struggled financially, they faithfully tithed ten percent of their monthly income to the televangelists who smiled reassuringly back at them on their TV screens.

These carefully-manicured personalities were Christ's messengers, and they had the gold and jewels to prove their favored status. Heck, these people didn't even have to promise heavenly VIP lounges to extract their ten percent from the faithful masses— they were well-financed professionals who made the Mormons look like a cheap circus side-show. The obvious hypocrisy underlying these evangelists' materialism didn't seem to bother my family. What need did they have for accomplishments or possessions when this world was merely an impermanent portal to the next?

Though I was now an adult, and it should have been easy to cut ties with these people and move on with my life, they were my family, and I loved them. How could I be happy watching them waste their lives pursuing what I believed to be a farfetched fairy tale from the Bronze Age? Just as they sought to save me from Satan's hell, I was determined to save them from their fate of hell on earth. It wasn't merely altruism—my own happiness was also on the line. It's hard to keep a steady girlfriend when your relatives follow a Sloppy Joe dinner with a casual round of casting out demons.

The only book I ever saw my grandfather read was the Holy Bible, but when he died I discovered that he had left a massive collection of books in his garage. No one in my family seemed to have any interest in the books, so when the lawyers managed his estate, I had free reign to take as many volumes as I wanted. One day while paging through a volume by Henry David Thoreau, I read a passage that addressed my dilemma. "If you would convince a man that he does wrong, do right. But do not care to convince him. Men believe what they see. Let them see."

I was young, highly ideological, and impetuous, so that day I took Thoreau's advice—literally. I was going to show my family the error of their ways, and the best way I knew how was to quit my job, give away all of my possessions, and study every spiritual discipline until I found the one, irrefutable path to salvation. I no longer remember the exact number of days, but I spent the greater part of six months living out of my car, sleeping in parks, and stereotypically, spending one night in a Nebraska cornfield. I passed the days in libraries and bookstores, reading every religious document I could find.

But each new book provided more questions than answers. Most of the major religions claimed to be the only path to salvation, but I found irreconcilable problems with all of them. Discouraged, I began compiling their similarities. Ultimately, I discovered that every major religion, and almost every form of spirituality, promotes some iteration of the Golden Rule as a guiding principle of morality. As Kurt Vonnegut once said, "Goddammit, you've got to be kind." I wondered if that was as good as it was going to get. But somehow I knew that the Golden Rule was never going to be enough to satisfy my family. Their supposed salvation had made them self-righteous, and I decided that if I was going to sway their minds, I needed to present them with an alternate interpretation of their own scriptures.

One day, while browsing through a bookstore for The Answer, I found the explanation for what they were missing. Of all people, it came from Hazrat Inayat Khan, a Muslim who, according to them, was going to burn in Hell. He said:

It is this awakening of the soul that is mentioned in the Bible. Unless the soul is born again, it cannot enter the Kingdom of Heaven. Being born again means that the soul is awakened after having come on earth, and entering the Kingdom of Heaven means that this world, the same kingdom in which we are standing just now, turns into Heaven as soon as the point of view has changed. Is it not interesting and most wonderful to think that the same earth we walk on is earth to one person and Heaven to another? And it is still more interesting to notice that it is we who change it; we change it from earth into Heaven, or we change it otherwise. This change comes not by study, nor by anything else, but only by the changing of our point of view.

I was blown away. The quote perfectly articulated my exact feelings in a way I had never been able to express myself. Once I dropped this shitstorm of wisdom on my family's next Bible study, they'd be able to have a holy bake sale for the record books. I took pleasure in imagining the looks on their faces as I forced them to question the very bedrock of their belief system. When they realized that I was correct, they would name children after me. I would be a godfather five times over. I imagined that they might even remake the family crest to depict me in a suit of armor, gloriously raising a shimmering blade of spiritual truth toward the heavens.

For the first time since I started my quest for spiritual insight, I experienced true happiness. The burden that had been shackled to me since my childhood was gone. Everything now seemed so different to me—the trees, the sky, the stars—everything had a deeper and more tangible radiance. I no longer resented my family for exposing me to their faulty belief system. I now had empathy for them. They didn't invent these irrational tales of salvation and damnation. Someone had taught these scriptures to them, too—undoubtedly when they were innocent and impressionable children. I wondered what my source of joy was, and if I could share it with them. I felt like I had been given a fresh start, like I had been born again.

Could it be? Could the concept that had caused me so much childhood anxiety now be responsible for my newfound happiness? I resisted the conclusion, afraid that I might fall victim to the same dogma that had enslaved my family.

But this was different. I had never looked to the heavens for my happiness. I was simply realizing once again what I had understood as a child: the only heaven I'll probably ever know is right here, and right now. Accepting Jesus into their hearts was supposed to have incited similar feelings of divine reverie, but it clearly didn't work. Despite all of the flailing arms and talking in tongues, they had the born again thing all wrong. As before, I wanted to help my family—to save them from their fate—but I remembered Thoreau's wisdom. "Let them see."

And that's what I've tried to do ever since. I've come to accept that my rational arguments will never sway the hearts and minds of my family. They still profess to hold the key to God's divine love and wisdom out of one side of their mouths, while condemning others with their hateful rhetoric out of the other. Some of them casually pass me off as a crazy atheist, while others hold out faith that this "lost sheep" will one day return to the fold. But just because I haven't chosen a religious path to follow does not mean that I am lost. I've simply taken their advice and placed my chips on Pascal's table.

I'm betting that if there is a God who created the mountains, he or she would rather have me spend my Sunday afternoon breathing in the sweet mountain air than squeezing in between overweight, flatulent parishioners in an uncomfortable church pew. I'm betting that if there is a God, he or she has a sense of humor and will think that teaching my little cousins how to make fart noises during Sunday school is a more worthwhile endeavor than helping them memorize ancient scriptures some bible scholars scarcely understand. I'm wagering that if there is a God, he or she designed sex to feel good, and that I'll be a better person from regularly performing what most Christians would consider unspeakably perverse lovemaking acts to my wife than by living a chaste life with a bunch of hairy social outcasts in some remote monastery in the Himalayas.

And if my wife and I decide to have a family, I'm betting that if there is a God, he or she will prefer that I spend every free minute of my time making sure that our precious children feel as much love during their time on this planet as humanly possible. I'll look into their eyes and know that they are perfect—that original sin is a lie. I'll know that they were born right the first time. When they get older and inevitably ask me what happens when we die, I'll tell them the truth—that I've spent more time than most trying to answer that question, and that I'll never be certain. I'll tell them that a lot of people have many different ideas about God and Heaven—some crazier than others—and despite daddy's uncanny brain power, he hasn't been able to determine whose ideas, if any, are correct.

I'll say that I hope we live again, but that I'm honestly not sure. I'll tell them that if there is a God who created and loves us, what he or she probably wants more than anything is for us to fiercely and passionately love one another as if today is the last day we'll spend together on this extraordinary planet. I won't fill their heads with tales of demons and damnation in order to indoctrinate them towards or away from any particular religious or spiritual tradition. Even if they jump on the next spaceship to planet Kolob to take bong rips and play beer pong in Heaven's VIP lounge, I'll still think that they are perfect. And no person, and certainly no god, will ever convince me otherwise.

Fatman & Robbin'

...When my dad broke the news to me that we weren't going to have any presents for Christmas, I was surprisingly unshaken. I was more concerned about the fate of my grandpa, and I quickly went to work on a new drawing for him. After two hours of laborious sketching and shading—making sure every detail was just right, I was finally finished. I walked alone down the hallway of the intensive care unit, and when I made it to his door, I was surprised to see that for the first time since his arrival, he was alone. He looked tired and beaten, and I was scared to look at him at first. "Grandpa?" I cautiously whispered, afraid that he might not answer...

I was born into a life of privilege. You would not know it by looking at the current state of my family, but at one point, however brief, we were somebodies. Around the same time the Allied Forces toppled Hitler and Mussolini, my great-uncle invented and manufactured the world's first pickup camper. And after nearly four years of armed conflict and over four-hundred-thousand fallen soldiers, Americans were ready to escape into the great outdoors for some rest and relaxation. Business boomed, and soon orders for new campers came in from all over the country.

By the time I was six-years-old, my great-uncle had acquired a huge manufacturing plant in a small town in eastern Idaho and was employing nearly everyone in my family, including my dad. On days when I went to work with my dad, I wandered around the manufacturing plant, watching the campers being built from the frame up. I would bring my superhero action figures and hide away in a remote corner of the facility, lost in the epic battles I created.

On particularly nostalgic days, I can still smell the hydraulic fluid and hear the echoes of pneumatic wrenches bouncing off the warehouse walls. This was the soundtrack of my childhood.

My father worked closely with my grandpa on the sales side of the business. They regularly traveled to trade shows across the country, and also managed a local sales lot in town. I spent many childhood days on the camper lot with them, playing with the latest action figures they brought back for me from their travels. I carried a sketch pad and a drawing pencil with me wherever I went, and I often spent my afternoons on the lot, drawing satirical cartoons of superheroes, family members, and friends.

Hulk Hogan, for example, might have been depicted as Hulk Hoagie, a muscle-bound pastrami on rye. Mr. T. was Mr. Tee'd off—a gold chain wearing, high blood pressure having, angry, black golfer who only had one level of volume for his voice— LOUD. His caption? "I don't hate my caddy. I pity the fool."

One summer afternoon, my dad was showing a fifth-wheel trailer to a couple from California. It must have been thirty-feet long, and came equipped with its own shower, tub, toilet, refrigerator, and mechanical blinds that shut with the push of a button. For 1985, this was the *crème de la crème* of recreational vehicles. It was one of my favorite trailers to stage superhero battles in, and though a sale of this size was always a good thing for the company, I didn't want to see it go. After five minutes or so of eavesdropping on my dad as he described the benefits of the trailer's foam-core insulation and other "Alaska Package" features, it was clear that the wife loved it. Her husband, a tall, burly man with sun-bleached hair, on the other hand, had some reservations.

"You know, Virgil," the man began. "We like you, and we really love this trailer, but I gotta tell ya, I'm not really happy about the headroom in the bathroom."

My dad's name is Virgil, middle name Ovid. With a name like that you would have thought that his mother was a Latin poetry scholar or some kind of academic type, but that couldn't be further from the truth. I've been to her trailer in Rupert, Idaho, and it's not exactly the birthplace of Socrates. Besides giving him that tragic name, she also commented in his baby book how "homely" a child he was as an infant. She was a real charmer, that one.

No, I don't think my dad's name was given to him out of a

love for poetry, for classical literature, or even for the boy himself. If I were a betting man, I'd wager that after a long night of drinking boxed wine with her fellow waitresses during her third trimester, she started fumbling through a dusty encyclopedia that one of her several ex-husbands had left behind, randomly opened it up to an entry for Latin poetry, stumbled upon the authors Virgil and Ovid, thought the names sounded "smart," and the rest, as they say, is history.

My dad, surprisingly, seemed to have survived his embryonic intoxication and the subsequent effects of growing up in this small town purgatory, mostly unscathed. He was, and still is, quite possibly the nicest guy on the face of the planet. I have never met a person who, after meeting my dad for the first time, didn't instantly feel genuine affection toward him.

Unfortunately, nice guys aren't always the best at being pushy and closing a sale. My grandfather, on the other hand, was a first generation Sicilian American who was as smooth and direct as they came. He could sell you your own tube socks if he really wanted to—I know, because he once used this trick to hustle me out of my allowance.

As he walked the sales lot that day, my grandpa overheard the man's complaints about the bathroom's lack of headroom, and he jumped at the chance to help my dad seal the deal with the burly Californian. I listened outside as my grandpa entered the trailer and immediately asked the man, "Excuse me sir, but what seems to be the problem?"

He asked the question without introducing himself, interrupting the large man mid-sentence, as if to say, "You're going to buy this trailer today, you huge fuck, or I'm going to put my size twelve, Italian leather boots up your free-loving, hippy ass."

"Well, we, uh...we like the trailer—we really do," the man stammered, unsure what to make of my grandpa and his intrusion. "It's just that I'm a tall guy and I have to bend over when I go into the bathroom because there's not very much headroom."

Amused, my grandfather looked the man up and down, clearly unimpressed by his size, and replied with a straight face, "What's the matter? You shit standing up?" The man stood there, stunned and silent, his lower jaw hanging wide open. It was as much an accusation as a question.

"Granted, it's been a while since I was in California," he continued. "But the last time I was there, people still took their shits sitting down."

If there is a comeback to that line of reasoning, we certainly did not hear it that day. Suffice it to say that the couple from California drove away with the trailer, much to the amusement of my grandpa. After they left, he sat in his office eating a jar of asparagus-flavored baby food. He had recently undergone radiation therapy for cancer, and had lost his sense of taste. The doctors were not sure if it would ever come back. As a Sicilian, it broke his heart to not be able to taste his wife's gourmet cuisine, but he resigned himself to the idea that it was probably a good idea to eat healthy foods until his sense of taste returned. Unlike his doctors, my grandpa had faith that he would once again taste oxtail stew and lasagna.

He sat in his leather-studded lounge chair that afternoon, carefully spooning out the green, tapioca-like sludge, a wide smile of satisfaction strewn across his broad face. I was very young at the time, but as I look back I remember him having that look quite often, as if he had been bestowed with some secret knowledge that he had no intention of sharing with the rest of us.

"That was pretty cool how you got that guy to buy that trailer today, Grandpa." I told him. "How did you do it?"

He paused for a moment and licked the green muck from his spoon, searching for the right words. "Well, Dolly, you know how you like to play with those superhero toys and draw pictures of them?" I nodded as I watched him replace the lid on the empty baby food jar. I never told him that "Dolly" was a girly thing to call a boy. "Well, your grandpa has super powers of his own."

"Really, grandpa?" I gullibly asked. "Could you teach me? I wanna be a superhero!"

He smiled, patted me on the back, and said "Sure, grandson, but not today. Your grandpa is tired. Why don't you go run along and make me another one of those beautiful pictures? You know how much your grandpa loves it when you make drawings for him."

My great-uncle, the founder and owner of the recreational vehicle business, owned an enormous estate on the shores of Lake Lowell. It was just up the road from one of Idaho's senators, in a development reserved for the state's wealthy elite. For a few years our family was regularly invited to high-class events at the senator's place, and sometimes his family even joined us at my great-uncle's residence. It was a true gentleman's mansion, equipped with the largest television I have ever seen, secret passages, a gigantic Koi pond, and a game room with the heads of virtually every beast you could think of. Behind the property was an outbuilding for his Olympic-sized swimming pool, featuring an electronic roof that opened like a football dome.

Adventures were never hard to come by in this child's fantasy land, even when one wasn't seeking excitement. During one of my great-uncle's elaborate dinner parties I frantically searched for a restroom, but all five of the bathrooms on the main floor were occupied by guests. In my desperation, I sprinted upstairs to my great-uncle's master suite. There I found my salvation: it was as if God had beamed down His own personal commode for me to use.

It was easily the most complicated toilet I had ever seen, with an array of confusing nozzles and knobs. It didn't even have a seat, but I was so desperate to relieve myself that I didn't mind squatting. After I finished, I pressed the button to flush, but instead of the water going down the hole like a normal toilet, it sprayed all over my new party clothes. Terrified and covered in filthy, excrement-laden water, I went screaming down the curved staircase of the stately home, thoroughly soaked, and convinced that God's toilet had attacked me.

I continued running and screaming until I reached the game room, where I came face-to-face with my great-uncle's newest addition to his collection: a massive, stuffed grizzly bear. The animal was standing erect on its hind legs, its terrible teeth exposed in a menacing expression of hunger. Terrified, I shrieked a cry of mortal peril, turned on the spot, and sprinted out of the game room and into the foyer where many of the guests were drinking cocktails and munching on appetizers. I was wheezing heavily, and I rested my hands on my knees for a moment to catch my breath before warning them, between sobs, of the imminent danger. I don't remember the exact words I used, but I said something to the effect of, "There's a killer toilet and a bear on the loose! Everybody run!"

As my charismatic great-uncle casually assured the guests that they were safe from diabolical latrines and grizzly bears, my grandpa took my hand and guided me upstairs to clean up. He explained to me that bidets were used for washing yourself up *after* doing your business.

"I know it's confusing, Dolly. Don't you worry about it. Some people apparently like to take their poops standing up. Others like to spray their butts with water after a good poop. None of it makes any sense to grandpa, either."

He then took me by the hand and led me to the mansion's toy room, which I feel confident in saying, easily contained the largest collection of toys in the state of Idaho at the time. Tragically, unless my cousins and I came over to use them, these toys lay around unused for most of their lonely existence, wasting away on luxurious kangaroo rugs from various safaris my great-uncle had taken. I was particularly jealous of a rare Batman action figure my great-uncle had acquired in Japan. Batman was always my favorite superhero, because he was just a normal guy, like my dad or my grandpa. Unlike Superman or Spiderman, who were both bestowed with extraordinary powers like super strength or flying, anybody could be like Batman if they really wanted to.

As grandpa and I acted out our fight scene with the Japanese Batman figurines, we had no idea that these days of plenty were coming to an end. Downstairs at the dinner party, my great-uncle was receiving terrible news. He and several others in the family, my grandfather included, had made a hefty investment in a proposed factory, which was no longer going to be built. The specific details about the investment were never a popular topic of discussion, even when I became an adult, so I never got a straight answer about it. Something about having an inside tip on a sugar-beet factory. Whatever it was, they bet terribly wrong, and as a result, my great-uncle's company had to shut down.

The company's downfall sent the family into a tailspin. Almost our entire extended family was working for the corporation one day, and the next they were unemployed. We all lost everything: houses, cars, boats—even our beloved campers. While a handful remained in Idaho, most of the family, in their infinite wisdom, eventually made their way to Nebraska where several of my mother's siblings resided.

Shortly after the company's demise, my grandfather bought a small, model home on the outskirts of Omaha. The mailbox still had "Brochures" painted across its side from when it was used to hold informational flyers for the development. My grandpa had apparently left some hefty debts back in Idaho, because I remember bill collectors calling soon after he moved in. One actually showed up to his house one day when I was visiting.

"Hello, Sir. Are you Mr.—"

"Brochure," My grandpa interrupted. He pointed to the mailbox with a wide smile. "We're the Brochures. Can I offer you some coffee? Perhaps a slice of bundt cake?"

The man turned and walked toward his parked car in the street, clearly disappointed. My grandpa smiled at me with the same grin as the day he sold that trailer to those people from California. After the company's failure, he had suffered two heart attacks, one after the other. But he still looked as strong and vibrant as ever to me. Plus, he had regained his sense of taste, and was eating everything he could get his hands on. As long as my grandpa had good food and his family around, it seemed nothing could get him down.

"Come on, Dolly, let's go inside. I think your grandma's nearly finished with the pasta, and I'd love to see some of those drawings you've been working so hard on."

Around the same time the bill collectors came calling for my grandpa, my parents moved us into a two bedroom apartment next to Interstate 80, not far from my grandparents. It was one of those places where, if you were quiet and listened closely, you could hear the steady hum of the passing cars, no matter the time of day. Fortunately—or unfortunately—depending on how you looked at it, the couple in the apartment above us usually canceled out the highway noise with their incessant fighting and subsequent loud, raunchy make-up sex. My parents told me that they were just wrestling, but I wrestled with my cousins all the time and we never sounded anything like *that*.

Soon after our arrival, my dad started a hauling service with my uncle, who managed the city landfill. My uncle was an exceptionally kind man who loaned my dad his pickup truck and let him dump at the landfill for free. In exchange, he asked for a small piece of the profits once my dad was able to build up his clientele. As before, I went to work every day with my dad, this time helping him load brush, leaves, and any other junk people didn't want sitting around their houses anymore. It was hard work, but I loved it. Not only for the time I got to spend with my dad, but also for my three dollars a day salary, which I invested exclusively on comic books, baseball cards, and action figures.

Two months into the hauling business, things were off to a good start. My mother began working at a nearby fast-food restaurant for just over minimum wage, and her meager income, combined with what my dad made doing hauling and other odd jobs, was finally starting to make ends meet. Gone were the days of lake front-properties and parties with senators, but life was beginning to at least normalize.

Still, our misfortunes were not behind us. It started with my uncle's untimely death. As he drove into work one misty morning, just before daybreak, a semi-truck appeared out of the thick fog and slammed into his car. He was dead on impact.

With him gone, everything changed. My dad no longer had a business partner or a truck, and as a result, he no longer had an income. My mother's skimpy paychecks soon proved inadequate to pay the bills, and we began to struggle again. Even greater than the immediate financial repercussions of the loss of my uncle was the emotional and spiritual blow to the family. With his first son taken from him so suddenly, my grandpa suffered a third heart attack. The doctors said he would be lucky if he made it through Christmas.

On Christmas Eve my entire family spent the night at the

hospital, keeping watch over my grandpa. The pastor adminis-tered his last rites, and everyone said their goodbyes. But the stub-born old Sicilian refused to die on the birthday of his savior. I fell asleep next to my mom in an old leather recliner in the waiting room that night.

At around 3:00 a.m., my dad went to our apartment to grab some pillows and blankets, and a few presents for Christmas morning. When he arrived at our apartment, the door had been smashed open. The burglars had dumped the contents of our trash cans all over the kitchen floor, and once they were empty, the thieves used them to carry away every last food item from our cupboards. All of my mother's jewelry was taken, and the presents that lay beneath the tree just hours earlier were now all gone.

When my dad broke the news to me that we weren't going to have any presents for Christmas, I was surprisingly unshaken. I was more concerned about the fate of my grandpa, and I quickly went to work on a new drawing for him. After two hours of laborious sketching and shading—making sure every detail was just right, I was finally finished. I walked alone down the hallway of the inten-sive care unit, and when I made it to his door I was surprised to see that for the first time since his arrival, he was alone. He looked tired and beaten, and I was scared to look at him at first.

"Grandpa?" I cautiously whispered, afraid that he might not answer.

"Ryan, my Dolly," he whispered back in an exhausted, but cheerful rasp. With all of the tubes surrounding him he looked like a miserable Italian insect that had stumbled upon the hospital's inescapable web. Still, he managed a smile. "Come in, grandson. I've been missing you."

"I've been missing you too, grandpa. I made you a picture."

"Well, you know how I love your pictures, Ryan. Come here. Sit down, and let grandpa take a look at what you've made for him."

I addressed the picture:

To: Grandpa Brochure

Love: Your Dolly (Ryan)

It was entitled *Fatman and Robbin'*, and it depicted two criminals with masks robbing our apartment. "You see, grandpa, these guys aren't like Batman and Robin. Bruce Wayne's parents were killed when he was a little kid, and he decided to fight against crime, not become a criminal. They could never become superheroes like him."

I didn't know it at that moment, but it would be the last time that I would hear him laugh. It was a deep, hearty bellow that echoed throughout the ward. "Well, isn't that a riot? You're something else, my grandson. You know your grandpa is very proud of you and loves you very much, right?"

"Yes, grandpa."

A smile moved across his pale face. It was that familiar grin.

"You remember that time when grandpa told you about his super powers?"

"Yes, grandpa."

"Well, what would you say if I wanted to tell you that secret right here, right now?"

"Right now? Really?"

"Really. Come here, Dolly. It's very secret, so I've got to tell you in your ear. Only the truest of heart can possess the secret, so it's very important that no one else can hear. Your grandpa isn't going to be around forever, and you're going to have to fill his shoes one day."

It was the most bittersweet moment of my young life.

I eagerly crawled up on the bed and leaned in close against his warm chest, careful to make sure no one else could hear. The nurses and doctors in the hallway had no idea that a dying superhero was passing on his secret powers to his loyal sidekick.

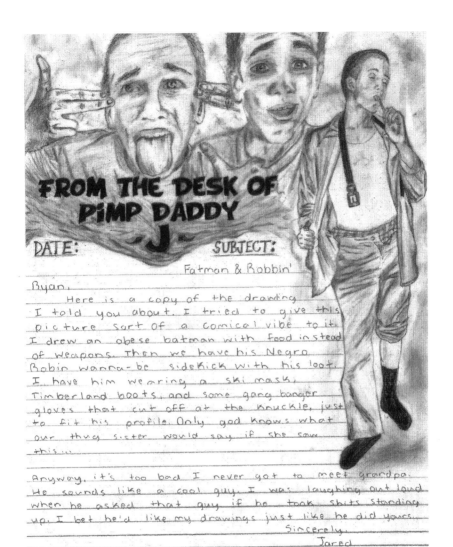

FROM THE DESK OF PIMP DADDY "J"

DATE: _____ SUBJECT: _____

Fatman & Robbin'

Ryan,

    Here is a copy of the drawing I told you about. I tried to give this picture sort of a comical vibe to it. I drew an obese batman with food instead of weapons. Then we have his Negro Robin wanna-be sidekick with his loot. I have him wearing a ski mask, Timberland boots, and some gang banger gloves that cut off at the knuckle, just to fit his profile. Only god knows what our thug sister would say if she saw this...

Anyway, it's too bad I never got to meet grandpa. He sounds like a cool guy. I was laughing out loud when he asked that guy if he took shits standing up. I bet he'd like my drawings just like he did yours.

                Sincerely,
                Jared

Amber Anderson

It was the beginning of the seventh grade, and I was the new kid in junior high. I would have challenged an angry water buffalo to a mud wrestling match if it meant making some new friends and impressing a pretty girl. But not just any pretty girl—I had one particular girl in mind. Her name was Amber Anderson.

I had moved from across town a couple of months before, and despite my desperate displays of affection—volunteering to wash off her paint tray in art class, letting her cut in front of me in the lunch line, and moving to a different table so she could sit next to her friends in the cafeteria—Amber still had no idea I existed. Though I probably had a better chance of beating that water buffalo, I was determined to do whatever it took to become one of the cool kids and make Amber my girlfriend.

At the end of each school day, several dozen of the coolest kids from seventh and eighth grade bundled up in expensive winter clothes and made their way down the road to Bronco's Burger Shack. There they smoked cigarettes and drank whatever booze they had managed to smuggle from their parents' liquor cabinets. No one ever officially invited me to these after-school get-togethers, but that didn't discourage me from attending. The politics of junior-high popularity have always been as complicated as honey-bee mating rituals, and if you want a shot at the queen, you have to be assertive.

With that in mind, I walked down to the restaurant, found Amber standing outside, and without a word, coolly leaned up against the wall beside her. I had spent hours in front of the mirror at home practicing this James Dean pose—equal measures of stoic, dour, and impenetrable—which, of course, are all slight variations of the same thing: detachment. So, I was going to be assertive...but detached. No one ever claimed that teenage boys were the most logical humans walking the planet.

I was only twelve-years-old and had never been drunk before, but when Amber took a sip of brandy and blindly passed the bottle to me, I didn't think twice before taking a monster-sized gulp. I figured the drunker you got, the cooler everyone would think you were. The liquor was disgusting and it burned my throat on the way down, but I promised myself I wouldn't look like a nerd and spit it out. Before I passed the bottle along, I made a sound that was something between the refreshed "ahh!" you make after taking a drink of soda, and the emasculated "argh!!!" of getting kicked in the nuts.

I pretended that I sounded cool, quickly regained my steely exterior, and carefully studied Amber for a few minutes. She was tall—just a couple of inches shorter than me, and she had the shiniest, silkiest blonde hair I had ever seen. The bottoms of her jeans were shredded from years of wear, and to me, they epitomized all that was cool. She wore a pair of winter boots with faux-fur accents, which matched the furry hood of her winter coat. Under her coat I could see part of a Kurt Cobain t-shirt, which completed her grunge rock look.

The warm air escaping from her moist, red lips turned to vapor with each exhale. I found myself wanting to reach out and touch those lips more than anything in the world. Her eyes were a captivating green with a band of light hazel in the center, and when she looked at you, she really looked at you. At least that's what I had heard—she had scarcely looked in my direction since I started going to this new school.

The bottle of brandy circled around the group two more times, and after my third gulp I was beginning to feel its effects. It was then that the unthinkable happened: Amber Anderson—without anyone holding a gun to her head or anything—actually spoke to me.

"So, you're that new kid, right?" She asked with her cool, grunge-girl diction. "What's your name, Ray or...Ron or something, right?"

"It's Ryan," I passively said in my best James Dean, as if her question were an inconsequential leaf blowing by in the breeze. I thought it best to keep my replies as brief as possible.

"Oh, yeah. That's right—Ryan. We've got art together, right?

You're the guy who likes to wash everybody's paint tray."

I shyly nodded and grunted a guttural affirmation. *The coolest girl in school kind of knows my name. And she noticed me in art class!* I thought. I was convinced that this was a breakthrough of epic proportions, but I couldn't let on how excited I was.

"Ryan, you don't have a smoke I could bum do ya? The stupid jerk at the gas station will only sell them to me if I make out with him, and he's totally gross, so that's not going to happen. And I'm, like, craving them *so* bad."

"Um, no, I don't. I'm sorry," I pitifully replied and looked down at the cracked asphalt of the recently-plowed parking lot. The one thing in the world she wanted at this moment was a cigarette, and I couldn't help her. There were thousands of dirt-bag truckers all over the country who had exactly what Amber Anderson needed, but all I had was five dollars in my pocket and dirty shoes. I succumbed for a moment to a haunting vision of a grizzly trucker happily pulling out his pack of Marlboro Reds and passing Amber a cigarette. *Thank you, Mr. Truck Driver. You've satisfied my craving, and now, as a reward, you can take your prize—my virginity.*

"That's OK," she said, snapping me out of my morbid day-dream. "I'm going to go ask around and see if anybody else has one I can bum." As she turned around, her golden locks reflected the afternoon sunshine on my face. If this were a cartoon, the "whoosh" of her hair would be chimed by the "zing!" of the xylophone striker sliding across eight, ascending notes in quick succession. The image of her hair flying over her shoulder would play back in slow motion, glazing my eyes over with slot machine hearts and making me a slave to her love spell. There's just something magical about a pretty girl swishing her hair. Rejects everywhere agree that it should be outlawed.

As she began to walk away, I managed to drunkenly stammer, "…But I can get some smokes for you…if you want. I mean—that is what you want right? Because otherwise you wouldn't have asked me for cigarettes—unless you wanted to smoke them, so I guess that you do want them, and I can get them for you, like no problem whatsoever. I can do that. Totally."

So much for keeping it short, I thought. Somewhere, James Dean was shaking his head in amused, but indifferent disbelief.

"Really?" She replied. "That would be so great. Are you sure it's not a hassle, because I can get my boyfriend or somebody to buy them later."

"Boyfriend? No, don't do him—I mean…that. No, I can definitely get you smokes. Just wait here for a minute. Don't go anywhere—I'll be right back."

"Awesome. That's really cool. You're so sweet, Ray."

Amber Anderson said I was sweet. *In your face, Mr. Truck Driver!* Never mind that she got my name wrong again. This truly was the best day of my life, except for one small problem—the cigarettes. How in the hell was I, a junior-high-schooler—nay—an intoxicated junior-high-schooler, going to get her a pack of smokes?

My twelve-year-old baby face more closely resembled Peter Pan than Captain Hook, so there was no chance anyone was going to sell me cigarettes without asking for I.D. This left stealing as my only option, which I had never done before. The gas station was only a block away from the burger place, so I didn't have much time to think over my strategy. This was to be my first time stealing, but that didn't mean I was completely inexperienced. *I did, after all, go to one of the roughest, low-income elementary schools in the state, and several of my friends there started stealing at an early age. Something must have rubbed off, right?*

As I approached the gas station, I thought back to my friend Nick's advice one morning when he had almost talked me into stealing baseball cards from Kubat's Pharmacy. "The trick to stealing is simple—you don't wanna just go stuffing your pockets with stuff and walk straight out the door," he barked in his matter-of-fact Italian American drawl. I remembered how his lazy lips slopped words together like wet ingredients in a mixing bowl. "That's what drunken homeless guys do in the winter when they *want* to get arrested. You're better than that, so act like it. Get comfortable. Browse the merchandise like you would on any normal day at the store. And most importantly, buy something. They never suspect anything when you buy stuff."

I checked my pant pockets for my unused lunch money. I had a headache over lunch, so instead of eating, I took a walk outside. *Thank god for that,* I thought, as I located the crumpled five dollar bill in my left pocket. The brandy had taken care of the headache, but now I had a different problem—*don't they keep cigarettes behind the counter?* Whenever my dad bought a pack he usually had to have the clerk get them. How was I ever going to get behind the counter?

To my relief, an answer presented itself as soon as I walked through the front door. Inside a round, metal display in front of the main counter were dozens of packs of discounted cigarettes—my holy grail. The attendant was nowhere to be found, so I quickly snatched up four packs and stuffed them into the pockets of my puffy winter jacket. As Nick had advised, I then made my way down the candy aisle to find something to buy. By the time I heard the clerk return from the stock room, I had already grabbed a couple pieces of taffy, a pack of gum, and a soda. I awkwardly staggered to the counter to purchase the items. My heart was pounding, and beneath my winter jacket I could feel the pits of my shirt becoming saturated with sweat.

The clerk wasn't the typical, stoner dropout you find at most gas stations. This guy was in his mid-thirties, had a full goatee, and dark, intelligent eyes like you might find on a crow. He looked like he owned the place, which made me even more nervous about the contraband stuffed in my pockets.

"That'll be three forty seven," he said after scanning my items. I felt certain he was studying every last detail of my pathetic junior-high exterior.

I handed him the money, snatched my stuff from the counter, and hurried toward the exit. I wanted to run out of there as fast as I could, but I knew that would give me away. Before I reached the door, the man called after me. "Not so fast, son." My heart sank. I was busted. *Oh my god! He knows!* I thought. *He's going to call the cops on me. They're going to send me to juvie jail and big, black kids are going to stab me with homemade shivs!*

My cousin once told me that kids in juvenile detention centers rub their toothbrushes against the brick mortar in their cells, grinding the ends into sharp points for stabbing little white runts like me for no other reason than, well, being little white runts. I imagined my epitaph: "Virgin Shoplifter Stabbed to Death with Improvised Toothbrush. Never Gets to Touch Amber Anderson's Boobs. Truck Drivers Laugh."

There's no way that's going to be on my gravestone. I told myself. *What should I do—should I run?* Nick never told me what to do when you got caught. I guess guys like him never got caught.

"Come here, son," the cashier commanded. I reluctantly walked toward him; shoulders slumped and head down, awaiting my fate. He eyeballed me up and down before saying a word. Though there was only one of him, he had the presence of many men, and I felt as if I were standing naked in front of a crowd of jeering principals. I was ready to confess my darkest secrets to him when he said, "You forgot your change. I still owe you a buck fifty-three. You in a hurry or something, boy?"

"No, sir. Well—yes…kind of, sir. You see, there's this girl, and she asked me to get her some smo—I mean, soda, and I really like her, and I just was trying to hurry back to see her. So, I guess I'll be going now, sir. Thanks, sir."

I grabbed the change and hurried out the door. I couldn't believe I had done it! *How did that work?* Just moments before, I was on my way to becoming a victim of a violent toothbrush stabbing, but now everything was going to be different. My epitaph might now read: "Late Bloomer Looked Cool While Smoking Cigarettes with Hot Girlfriend. Cool Kids and Truckers Envious."

However, as I rounded the corner, all of the joy from my fantasy was blasted out of me in an instant by a vicious punch to the stomach. The blow knocked me clean off my feet, and I found myself lying on my back, looking up at the face of a tall, lanky kid about four years older than me. "I saw you steal those cigarettes, punk. Now you're going to pay."

"I, *(cough)*…don't know what you're talking about," I muttered between gasps of breath. His punch had knocked all of the wind out of my lungs, and I could hardly talk, so I just lay there limp in the snow like a discarded banana peel.

"So, you want to do this the hard way, huh? Suits me just fine." The scarecrow-looking boy proceeded to rain down several more blows upon my face. When I felt blood flowing from my nose, I put my hands up and pleaded for him to stop.

"Okay, okay. Here you go." I tossed him two packs of cigarettes from my left jacket pocket and spat out about a teaspoon of blood. I remember thinking how much more brilliantly-red blood looks when it is your own, particularly when it's staining perfectly-white snow.

"That it?" He demanded, his right fist threateningly clenched above his head. He smelled like a barn stall, and I just wanted him off of me. I grudgingly pulled out a third pack and tossed it a few feet away, hoping that he would get off me to go pick it up. It occurred to me that this guy must be the same jerk Amber had talked about—the one that wouldn't sell cigarettes to her unless she made out with him. There was no way he was going to get the fourth pack from me. I had to fight a couple of bigger kids in elementary school (the kind that were probably using brick walls to grind toothbrushes into shivs at that very moment), and though I'd probably get my ass kicked worse than it already had been, I would fight this guy too if it meant getting the chance to present Amber with her cigarettes. No one was going to mess that up for me.

"Very good," he said with a devilish grin as he got off my chest. "Now that wasn't so hard, was it, kid?" As I stood up to leave, he made it clear he wasn't done with me. "Where d'ya think you're goin'?" He snapped. He opened up a pack of the stolen smokes and lit one up. "You listen to me," he said with the cigarette dangling between his lips, "unless you want me to call the cops, you're going to come here next Thursday afternoon with fifty bucks, cash. If I'm not at the counter, ask for Billy. You don't show, I call the cops." He then made me write down my name, address, and phone number on a piece of paper.

I pulled myself out of the blood-stained snow and headed back to the restaurant to find Amber. It felt like Billy had detonated plastic explosives in my gut. Blood was still streaming from my throbbing nose, but despite my injuries, Amber was all I could think about. During the walk back, I thought about what it would be like to kiss her. I happily wondered if sharing a cigarette was close to the same thing as a kiss. After all, her lips would touch the cigarette and so would mine, so that's pretty close to first base, right? Maybe a bunt?

I didn't think my stomach could hurt much worse, but when I got back to the restaurant and saw Amber smoking a cigarette with another guy, a bomb worse than Billy's went off inside of me. Still recovering from the explosion, I approached her.

"Hey, Amber, I got your smokes," I said, my stupid grin exposing my blood-coated teeth. I opened up the pack of cigarettes, and though I had never smoked before, I pulled one out for myself.

"Oh my god, Ray—I mean, Ryan. What happened to you?"

She looked concerned. Some of her popular friends standing nearby looked impressed, which boosted my confidence.

"Oh, it's no big deal. I got caught stealing these." I proudly brandished the blood-stained pack, letting the light reflect off its cellophane wrapper as if it were Excalibur and I had pulled it from the stone just moments before. I wiped off a crimson smear before clumsily dropping the pack into her hands. "The guy at the gas station—you know, the jerk who tried to make out with you—he tried to get them back from me, but I wouldn't let him have 'em. They're for you." I must have looked something like a barn cat proudly presenting its horrified eight-year-old owner with a freshly-killed mouse.

"Wow. You got into *a fight* just to get me some cigarettes? I... don't know what to say. Thanks?" Suddenly, the boy next to her stood up, glared at me, grabbed Amber by the hand, and started pulling her in the opposite direction. "Come on, babe. Let's get outta' here."

"Well, I guess I'll see you at school on Monday, ok?" She yelled over her shoulder as her boyfriend dragged her away. *Goddamn caveman.* Amber looked worried, or disturbed. I couldn't tell which.

"Wha—Whaddya mean?" I said, shocked. "Where are you going? I mean, don't you wanna smoke one with me?" I lit the cigarette I had taken from the pack, inhaled, and violently coughed. My knees felt wobbly, my stomach was cramping, and for a moment, I felt a tear well up in my eye.

She freed her arm from her barbarian boyfriend and walked back towards me. "Um, I'm really sorry, but we're going back to

Jake's house to drink some more. It *is* Friday, you know. I'd invite you over, but he doesn't know you, and he and his friends can be kind of tough on kids they don't know—especially junior-high kids.

Besides," she said, surveying the damage to my face, "it looks like you've already had a pretty rough day..." She could see the look of devastation on my face, and continued in an optimistic tone. "...But I'll see you on Monday, okay? Thanks again for the smokes. That was really...uh, nice."

As I lay in bed that night, I decided that I hated Amber Anderson as much as I hated getting drunk off cheap brandy, choking on bargain cigarettes, listening to the taunts of hypothetical truck drivers, and getting blackmailed by white-trash gas station clerks who punch you in the stomach when you're not looking. I didn't need any of them. What I did need was a way to make fifty dollars by Thursday, and I tossed and turned all night trying to come up with ideas.

When I went upstairs for breakfast the next morning, the answer to my crisis was waiting for me outside on the ground: fresh snow—a lot of it. "You know," my dad said over the paper he was pretending to read so as to not be obligated to talk to my mother, "you should dust off the old shovel and make yourself some money today."

"You know what, dad?" I said with a genuine smile. "That's a great idea. That's exactly what I'll do."

For two-days-straight, I marched up and down the icy streets of my neighborhood, asking my neighbors to let me shovel their driveways. By the end of the first day, I had finished six driveways at ten dollars a piece. But I wanted to make more money, just in case Billy tried to jack up the price at the last minute, so I shoveled eight more driveways the following day. But I only received payment for seven of them—Mrs. Jackson never paid me for any of the work I did for her. Not with money, at least.

Mrs. Jackson was a widow who lived five houses down from ours, and she was well-known throughout the neighborhood because she told anyone who would listen that the government had bugged her home. It would typically go something like this: "Hello, Mrs. Jackson, it's a pleasure to meet you. How do you do?"

"Well, I'd be a helluva goddamned lot better if those Communists would stop listening to my phone calls," she'd say in a strained whisper, looking suspiciously up and down the block, presumably for an unmarked van with a long antennae poking out the roof. I had mowed her lawn several times the previous summer, and she always spoke to me in a whisper, fearful that the CIA had nothing better to do than to eavesdrop on the conversations of a prepubescent kid and his demented neighbor. The story was always the same: she didn't have any money to pay me, but she could whip me up something to eat. Foolishly, I had once accepted what looked like road-kill meatloaf as payment for trimming her hedges, and spent the rest of the day repenting at the porcelain altar. I wasn't going to make that mistake again.

"Don't worry, Mrs. J." I quietly whispered in her ear. I looked around to make sure no secret agents were lurking in the bushes.

"This one's on me." I studied the misshapen silhouette beneath her haggard nightgown, wondering if one day, long ago, she had been somebody's Amber Anderson. If Amber was going to look like that someday, why was I so intimidated by her?

"You're such a sweet boy," she said, adjusting her outdated bonnet. "I'll bet you've got to carry around a stick everywhere you go to beat the girls off you." I could deal with the conspiracy theories, but it was comments like this that made me think she was crazy.

When Monday morning came, I happily counted my money—one hundred and thirty dollars in all. I had more than enough to pay off Billy, with a bunch left over. *It's too bad Amber has a boyfriend.* I thought. *I might have bought her something nice with all of this money. Maybe a necklace or a ring—something to let truck drivers everywhere know that she belongs to me.*

But I couldn't forget that she had ditched me, and I was determined to ignore her. This shouldn't have been difficult, given the fact that until a few days before, she didn't even know my name. However, we did have several classes together, and I usually spent half of each period dreamily staring at her from across the room, trying to repress the trademark erection that makes wearing sweatpants to school impossible for adolescent boys everywhere.

But no matter what elaborate fantasies I dreamt up, they were still just that—fantasies. Girls like Amber Anderson didn't kiss, much less date, guys like me. Girls like her let nerds like me get their asses kicked by thugs at the gas station and then leave them to lick their wounds while they go off with their stupid, muscle-bound high-school boyfriends to get drunk and party. *Girls like her grow up to be scientists who perform agonizing experiments on puppies,* I convinced myself.

The week passed quickly, and soon it was Thursday. When the bell for the last period rang, I checked my pocket for the money. I brought fifty dollars, plus a twenty-five dollar back-up, just in case Billy tried to pull any stunts. On my way out of school, I saw Amber talking with a few of her friends. She noticed me, and I quickly turned and walked outside. I felt like an idiot about what had happened the previous week, and had no desire to relive my humiliation.

Once outside, I leaned against the brick wall of the school, closed my eyes, and took a few deep breaths. When I opened my eyes, I was surprised to see Amber standing in front of me, staring at me with those brilliant, green eyes. She stood there for several seconds, thoughtfully staring into my eyes. I didn't dare speak and interrupt the moment, so I just stared right back. After a few more seconds, she gently took my hand without a word and led me behind the school. There was an urgency in her footsteps, as if some celestial event—maybe an eclipse—was only minutes away, and she didn't want to miss it. She didn't want *us* to miss it.

As it did when I stole the cigarettes, my heart raced, but much faster this time. I didn't know what to expect, but I felt that something new and exciting was about to happen. Either that, or she was leading me to a royal beating, courtesy of her brawny boyfriend and his high-school friends. When we reached the back of the school, Amber stopped next to a row of tall pine trees. She softly, but firmly pushed me against the wall. Looking directly into my eyes, she leaned in slowly. *Was she going to…kiss me?*

While excited, I was still wary. The situation reminded me of a hunting show I had seen on TV. Elk hunters put out female elk decoys during mating season to lure in the bucks. Once the buck mounts the plastic decoy to mate, bam! The hunter hits him with an arrow through the chest. I resisted looking around, though I fully suspected that a high-school football player might jump out of the bushes any moment and sucker punch me.

But no one came. We were alone.

Her lips touched mine, softly and slowly. They were warm, moist, and slightly sweet, like when you eat a freshly-picked peach that's been hanging all day in the sunshine. She then placed her hands gently on each side of my face, drawing me in even closer as she put her tongue *inside my mouth.* I rested my hands on her hips, and we continued to embrace. Every thought in my mind disappeared, and all I felt was warmth. Before I knew what was happening, Amber silently stepped back, looked me over one last time, and walked away without a word. I tried to call after her, to follow her, but neither my voice nor my feet would obey my commands. I let myself slide down the brick wall until I was sitting in the muddy snow beneath the pine trees. I sat there in the snow for over an hour, trying to comprehend what had just happened to me.

On my long walk home, I thought of the perfect use for the rest of the money I had earned from shoveling snow—I decided to take my parents out to dinner to celebrate. Our favorite pizza place, Big Fred's, was very close to Billy's gas station, so I asked my dad if we could stop there before dinner so I could get some candy. He needed to fill up the gas tank anyway, so he agreed.

I volunteered to pump the gas and pay inside while the family waited in the warm car. Once inside, I saw Billy at the counter and passed him an envelope. Inside was a note. It read:

Dear Asshole,

I was going to pay you the money, but then I realized that if you called the police on me, they probably wouldn't like the fact that you had blackmailed and assaulted a twelve-year-old kid. Also, your boss probably wouldn't be pleased to learn that you kept the cigarettes I stole. So, basically, you're screwed.

P.S. – I made out with Amber Anderson, and it was AWESOME. Fuck you, loser!!!

For a moment, Billy looked like he might jump the counter and give me another pounding. His hands were clenched into angry, bony fists, and his chest heaved violently with each short breath he snorted through his nostrils. I was scared, but I found the courage to keep looking him in the eye. I also made my hands into fists, and waited for him to make his move. He might win, but at least he wasn't going to catch me off-guard this time. But the more I stared at Billy, the less fearful I became. I looked into his eyes, and for a moment, I felt an odd sort of kinship with him.

He reminded me of some of my fatherless friends at my old elementary school—a hard-knock group of boys who secretly wanted nothing more than to catch a pop-fly off the end of their fathers' baseball bats. Though they often got into fights to maintain their tough reputations, as you got to know them you quickly realized that none of them particularly enjoyed fighting. If Billy was anything like these boys, his life had been one long, interconnected string of failures. He was defeated again this night, and as he glanced down at the note in his trembling hands, I could tell that he knew it. He crumpled up the piece of paper and threw it at the trash can behind the counter, missing badly.

I stared at the balled-up note on the floor and felt bad for Billy. But my pity quickly yielded to a new feeling. I had gotten the girl—though not in the way I had imagined. And I had defeated my enemy—though not by force. I considered myself part of that rag-tag group of boys to which Billy clearly belonged. But it seemed that my luck was changing.

I turned my back to Billy and walked out into the cold winter night. If this were a movie, I might have bumped shoulders with a muscular man on my way out the door. I would easily knock him out of the way as I continued my uber-cool, slow-motion strut towards my parents' station wagon. In reality, as cool and liberated as I felt that night, I probably looked like the awkward, hunched-over nerd that I was. But this nerd, despite all odds, made out with the prettiest girl in school. And that's the sort of thing that sticks with a guy forever.

Jack's Lions

A man named Thor once split my head open with a crowbar. Most people initially think I'm joking when I say this, but I read the police report—it clearly said his name was Thor. Yes, there exists a man in this world whose first name is Thor, and he apparently wanders around the Midwest, ruthlessly clobbering random strangers in the head with crowbars. I've told this story on countless occasions, mostly because, well, it's a really cool story. When it comes to storytelling, I'm the biggest one-upper out there. It's a character flaw, I know, but let's be honest, if you were assaulted by the Norse God of Thunder; you probably wouldn't shut up about it either.

The blood-filled story of me getting my head bashed in by a hammer-wielding god of destruction is my bread and butter. Even if it's the only story I tell all night, it's a guaranteed ticket to instant admiration with even the stuffiest of new acquaintances. Plus, it makes me sound like a badass, and when you're a having a rough day, there's nothing like making a crowd of people fear that you might kung fu the shit out of their asses if they don't laugh at your jokes.

Why this man thought it was a good idea to swing a crowbar at other human beings' heads that day still eludes me, but I do remember quite vividly how it all unfolded. The story begins on a warm, late-summer afternoon in Nebraska, which I've decided is the last stronghold on the planet for corn-cob foam hats and inbred swine named Thor.

I had dropped out of college a year earlier and was in-between apartments and ideologies at the time. So, I had been crashing on my cousin Jack's couch while I figured out my next move. The Nebraska Cornhuskers were still in their heyday of college-football domination, and my stoner buddy Dan and I were looking forward to watching the first game at Jack's apartment. We made a pre-game checklist:

"Lots and lots of pot?"

"Check."

"World-renowned chicken finger subs from Buffalo Company, extra ranch?"

"Check."

"Jell-O Pudding Pops—chocolate, vanilla, and swirl?"

"Check."

"You sure about that, bro?" I demanded. "If you mess with my pudding pops I'll go Cosby all over your ass."

"Roger that." Dan responded. "J. E. L. L. O. pudding pops are a go."

"Jack?"

"Che—Dude, where is Jack, man?" Dan asked.

The only thing missing from this apartment was its tenant, and we were too high to remember where he had gone. "Um, dude, I think he, like, went to get some Zingers, man," Dan guessed.

"Zingers?" I muttered with disdain. "Who eats Zingers in the summertime? Honestly, have you smoked all of your brain cells away?"

Raspberry Zingers remain one of my favorite Hostess snacks, besides fried Twinkies and Chocodiles, of course, and there are strict protocols involving the season and time of day when they can be consumed. Jack would have agreed with me, wherever he was.

Jack was an interesting character—an enigma, really. He was what a movie narrator might call a warrior poet. Had he been born five centuries earlier, he would no doubt have been a knight or a rebel—a brave commoner who saved damsels from the clutches of evil counts and lords. He would have been celebrated by the simple people of the countryside and feared by the noblemen who exploited them. Jack should have been the kind of folk hero you saw in the movies, clad in a Scottish kilt or a suit of armor, blood-stained and terrifying. Instead, he was born in Nebraska in the bustling twentieth century, filled with its carbon-copy strip malls and equally uninspired sorority girls.

Jack always seemed out-of-place in the modern world, and though most people dismissed him as a social outcast, I knew better. I saw the warrior Jack—a man with lions in his heart, roaring and rattling their cages to get out. He was a noble creature the world should have revered. Instead, they threw five-cent peanuts and insults at him through the bars of his heart's cage.

That type of treatment wears a man thin, and after a while Jack put less and less stock in societal norms. He was bound to say anything that crossed his mind without thinking twice, so introductions and formal affairs were somewhat challenging.

"How'd you like those bitches, Rye bread?" He might say to me at a bar after meeting a group of girls. He would have on the same grease-stained shirt he wore to change his truck's distributor the previous day, along with snug-fitting Levi's, over which his hairy, melon-shaped belly hung. A pair of high-top Reebok sneakers and an Atlanta Falcons ball cap might complete the ensemble. "I bet you'd bend that blonde over and give her some of your limp linguini." He'd thrust his hips and make grunting noises until half of the bar was staring at us.

"Yes, Jack," I'd begin. "Now that you mention it, Suzy—that's her name—she is rather attractive. However, given the fact that she's standing right behind you, and just heard what you said, I'm reasonably confident that I won't be giving her anything tonight. On second thought, maybe I'll give her your number so she can call and tell you what a doucher you are."

Despite his social inadequacies, Jack was as fiercely loyal a friend as anyone could ask for. And in a scrap, you wouldn't want anyone else on your side. Beyond his dozen or so years of martial-arts training, Jack had something of a God-given knack for inflicting pain on others. I know this because, growing up, he and his older brothers would practice putting me in their favorite wrestling holds—the Boston crab was by far the most agonizing, and my most feared. We had been in plenty of fights together when we were young (there's not much else to do in the middle of the Great Plains), so when Jack came bursting through the front door of his apartment that afternoon, I knew immediately from the look in his eyes that we were about to be in another scrap.

It must have been the second week of August, as it was still very warm outside and the college football season was just beginning. But I couldn't help noticing that Jack was brandishing an industrial-strength ice scraper in his right hand. It was the kind that measures the length of an adult femur and provides you with the leverage needed to hack through an inch of windshield ice, as is necessary on some January mornings in America's Heartland. He pointed that unusually long scraper at me and yelled, "You! I need you now! They're outside waiting for us."

This is the part of the story when I tell my audience around the campfire or at the cocktail party, "Now, for those of you who have never smoked pot, the absolute *last* thing you want to do when you are stoned is participate in any sort of violent activity. You are at one with the universe, striving for harmony with all life forms, video game consoles, and snack foods."

Then everyone laughs, and for a moment, I feel smart, funny, and accepted. This is usually a fleeting feeling, however, because Jack's image will inevitably pop into my head and interrupt my Zen with a resounding belch and an insult. He might call me a ball gazer—one who stares at human testicles for satisfaction.

I tried to rationalize with Jack after he burst through the door.

"Dude, what are you talking about? I don't want to fight anybody today. I did mention we have been taking bong hits, right? *Bong hits*, Jack. As in, I'm super stoned right now. What are you planning to do with that ice scraper anyway?"

"Hurry up, Rye Bread," he said, ignoring my question. "They've got my keys." Rye Bread. Ham and Cheese on Rye. Rhino. Jack would even call me Cleveland Steamer once in a while, but never, ever, under any circumstances, has Jack ever called me by my first name.

"Who has your keys?" I asked.

"The guys I flipped off," he shouted in a childishly impatient voice, as if the answer was abundantly obvious and I was some sort of inferior life form for not being able to read his mind.

"Dude, why would you flip somebody off and then give them your keys?" I said sarcastically. "That wasn't smart, man."

After a primitive cave-man gesture that I can only assume meant that I should go fuck a sheep, Jack went on to mumble something about how a guy in a truck threw a pop can out of his window, which then bounced off the pavement and hit Jack's truck. I let my weed-fueled imagination take over from here. I imagined both guys staring each other down, taunting one another about macho truck things I've never understood—like the size of their engines, gaskets, and gears. This exchange naturally led to middle fingers flying all over the place, and when you're a twenty-year-old Nebraskan and someone flips you off, the only natural response is to ready your trusty ice scraper for the inevitable street fight to come.

I like to imagine that there never was a pop can involved.

Instead, the guy in question was driving a Dodge pickup truck with a bumper sticker that said something like *Eats Chevy's, Shits Fords*. Given Jack's affinity for Ford trucks, it was only natural to yell an anally-specific insult at the driver, tell him he screwed his mother last night, and give him the bird. Nebraskans hold only two things in the highest regard: football and trucks. Insult their wife and they might let it slide, but make fun of their truck's towing capacity and fists will fly.

Whatever really happened on Jack's drive home, the reality was that these guys followed him to his apartment, and in his rush to quickly get inside, he dropped his keys in the parking lot. Now these Ford haters knew where he lived, what he drove, and potentially had his keys.

"Okay, Jack," I began. My head was fuzzy from the weed, and it took me a moment to locate the correct words. "I get it. Those guys never should have questioned the superiority of Ford's drive train—that was *wrong* of them. But I don't want to fight today, so please just go tell them you're sorry. If they have your keys, politely ask for them back, and let's go watch the game. Remember: no truck insults."

"What are you talking about, Rye Bread? This has nothing to do with drive trains.

"Sure it doesn't."

Despite having my senses seriously impaired by several hits from Jack's three-foot bong, I remember what happened next with remarkable clarity. Jack agreed to my "no truck insults" terms, so he and I exited the apartment door to locate his keys. Jack then approached the driver of the truck, and they began to talk. I stayed about ten car-lengths back, in an effort to appear non-confrontational. I studied the truck, and as I suspected, it was an older, beat-up Dodge with peeling blue paint. Behind it, being towed by one of those yellow, plastic ropes you'd use to tie a boat to a dock, was an even more beat-up Ford escort. This Ford actually looked like something had shit it out.

What seemed like several minutes passed. Both men seemed calm. *If something were going to happen, it would have happened by now,* I thought. As was the case with so many things in my teen years, I was gravely mistaken.

While Jack spoke with the driver of the Dodge, the few rusty cogs that were still turning in my inebriated teenage brain realized that I could not see the driver of the old Ford Escort. Clearly someone had to be steering the thing while it was being towed. But where were they? Something was off. At the moment of this realization, I saw a blur fly past the open space between the two vehicles. It was a large man running with two stick-like objects in his hands, making a beeline for Jack.

"Jack! Look out!" I yelled.

But he didn't hear me. His back was turned to the man with the weapons, so without thinking, I set off in a dead sprint toward them. They must have been at least thirty yards away from me, and I arrived too late for the first blow. *This psychopath just blindsided Jack in the back of the head with a crowbar!* I thought. Jack fell to the ground in a sickening heap, his head squirting blood like a grotesque fountain. He was unconscious, and had it not been for his convulsions, I would have wondered if he were still alive. There was more blood spilling onto the concrete than I had ever seen at one time in my life. I had never been more terrified.

Thor brought his crowbar over his head to swing again. He was aiming at Jack's head, which was helplessly resting on the concrete in what looked like a liter or two of cherry cough syrup. I was still running towards him at full speed, desperately unsure about what I would do when I got there. At the last possible second before Thor hit Jack once again, I jumped and knocked him over in what must have looked to bystanders like a Special Olympics version of a superman dive. Saturday Night Live fans may recall "Handy Man," the black superhero with cerebral palsy who defended the rights of the disabled. That's who I imagine I looked like when I dove into Thor's chest that day. I usually leave that part out when I'm telling the story at a party.

We both rose to our feet, that enormous son-of-a-bitch still holding both his crowbar in one hand, and what looked like a billy club in the other. *Who the hell keeps a billy club in their car?* I thought. I typically tell those few loyal listeners who haven't left to get another Appletini or a refill on their cheese dip, that in life-or-death situations people have reported time standing still, all of their senses being heightened, and having a general sense that everything was going to turn out OK.

I don't know what asshole made up that lie, because as I stared west, directly into the afternoon sun, and a man named Thor swung a crowbar at my face, all I wanted to do was cry like a little girl and run away.

I once took a single Karate class when I was six-years-old. Besides practicing roundhouse kicks over the tops of metal folding chairs for an hour, all I remember from the experience is the sensei telling me that I needed to cut my mullet and stop wearing neon colored shirts if I wanted to continue attending his dojo. When I describe the ensuing fight sequence to an audience, I don't tell them that I renounced Karate that day and rocked my mullet for many years and Guns N' Roses concerts afterward.

Instead, I tell them that I have some mixed martial arts experience, all of which came rushing back to me in the split-second the crowbar zoomed towards my head. As Thor swung his crowbar, I swung my fist. We both connected, but *he* was the one that went down. I go on to describe how I quickly gained side control, and put him in an Anaconda choke. I'm careful to use as many technical fighting terms as possible. You'd be surprised how much you can learn about fighting by watching the Ultimate Fighting Championship on television.

These fighting terms give me credibility in case there's an actual tough guy listening in the crowd. I imagine myself telepathically threatening this imaginary skeptic in the group. "Oh yeah, I know all about Anaconda chokes, big man. Keep laughing at the jokes before you end up in one."

While on top of Thor, choking him out, I noticed that his face was covered in blood—a lot of blood. I took a sinister satisfaction in knowing that I had done that to him. *It serves him right for what he did to Jack,* I thought, squeezing his neck harder. But as I clutched Thor's tree stump of a neck, I saw several splatters of blood fall onto his face. The blood was mine, and it was flowing in a steady stream from a wound on the side of my head. Thor's crowbar had connected harder than I thought, and the guilty pleasure I took from choking him quickly turned to fear. I looked around for a moment, suddenly very aware of my surroundings. The fear I felt at the sight of Jack's helpless body had temporarily blinded me to what was happening, and I had no idea how our bloodbath had made its way into the middle of a busy street. People had started to gather around us, many of them on their cell phones—presumably with 911. I felt a sense of urgency to get the hell out of there.

Jack was starting to stir, and I could hear his groans from the other side of the road. He slowly began to stand up as my friend Dan made his way outside from Jack's apartment. Dan was happily whistling as he made his way towards us, but as he looked up and fully appreciated the gravity of the scene, his mouth fell open as if he were on a kindergarten field trip to the zoo and had just witnessed the slaughter of the world's last baby panda.

"Alright, asshole," I growled at Thor, "I don't know what you were thinking, you goddamn ogre, but you are lucky I don't get that crowbar and crack *your* head open. This is what is going to happen. I'm going to let you up. You are going to sit on that curb over there. If you move, you're in for a skull crushing. Got it?" He nodded without a word. I'm not sure if the behemoth half-breed even knew how to speak. For all I knew, his parents kept him chained to the wall in a secret room of their hideout like Sloth Fratelli in *The Goonies*.

I stood up and recited the license plate number of Thor's vehicle. "EKZ – 742. Dan, get over here and write this down," I barked. I could hear the wail of an ambulance in the distance.

Jack, for one, didn't need an ambulance. When I turned around, I saw that he had picked up Thor's crowbar and was chasing him around the street, cursing his mongrel mother with every stride. I heard Thor utter an effeminate scream right before Jack smacked him in the back of the head with the weapon. Next, Jack chased down Thor's accomplice, who had apparently been hiding in the bushes the whole time. The "crack!" of crowbar against this man's skull signified that Jack's vengeance was complete. In Norse mythology, Thor carries a short-handled hammer called a Mjöllnir, which when thrown, always comes back to him. *Maybe there is such a thing as karma,* I thought.

Soon the cops arrived, and after filing the police report, Jack and I went inside his apartment to dress our wounds before going to the hospital. The only things we could find that were big enough to wrap around our leaking heads were a pair of beach towels in Jack's closet. When we walked into the emergency room to get our MRIs, we looked like a small caravan of Middle Eastern men who had been in a desert scuffle; our tall, cone-shaped turbans leaking a trail of blood through the ER.

The MRIs revealed that neither of us had traumatic brain injuries, but the doctor suggested that we do something about the holes in our heads. Jack was the fortunate recipient of fourteen skull staples, while I, being lucky enough to have been struck by the "claw" end of the crowbar, only needed three. *All this over horsepower and payload capacity?*

Jack has never been known for handing out praise, so when he approached me in the hospital parking lot after getting stitched up, I fully expected him to say something like, "Hey, Rye Bread, you ball-licking butthole, thanks a lot for warning me before that cave-man hit me with that crowbar. Great job." But instead, he looked me right in the eye in a way he had never done before and said, "You know, if you weren't there today, I'd probably be a window licker in some institution." It was the only way he knew how to say thank you.

Jack and I haven't spoken much since the Thor incident. Truth be told, even though we spent many of our childhood years together, we've never been that close. We just never had very much in common. He likes working on engines on the weekends, and I'd much rather read Twain or Vonnegut. We're family, but sort of the same way a Chihuahua is a distant cousin of the Timber Wolf.

After a much-needed, decade-long hiatus from Nebraska, I recently returned for my dad's birthday party. It was the first time I had seen Jack for nearly ten years. I introduced him to my wife, and she excitedly shrieked, "You're the crowbar guy? Awesome! It's so great to meet you—I feel like I already know you." I've come to the conclusion that no matter how refined the person, everyone loves a good bloodbath story.

Jack still calls me Rye Bread. It's endearing. He now has a son, and though he still dresses like a grease monkey and comes up with the most random and revolting insults, he's much different than he was when we traded blood with Thor that day. We still don't have much in common, but he still looks at me the same way he did that day after the hospital. There is an unspoken understanding that, despite the years and the distance, still links us together. There is no doubt in my mind that if I were ever in trouble he would be there for me. And if I ever had to face another armed, mythological god to defend Jack or his affinity for Ford trucks, I'd do it again without hesitation.

If only for a short while, Jack's lions got out of their cages that day. It was just a street fight, so I don't expect everyone to understand why it was such a meaningful experience for me. The way I see it, it was one of the few opportunities Jack has ever had to unburden himself of the drab costume of civilization and become that fifteenth century warrior—to roar into the wind and smite his foe.

It was as if I was seeing Jack's true self for the first, and perhaps, only time. Maybe it was an echo of past nobility—a sign that our sterile civilization has not yet extinguished the warrior spirit that thrived in our ancestors; that maybe, down deep, we all carry lions inside of us. And if our lions are as magnificent as Jack's, there might be hope for us yet.

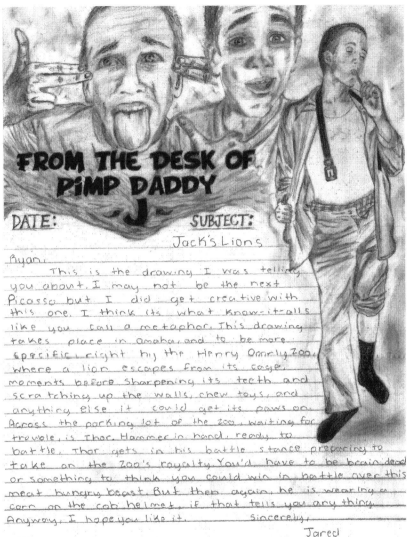

FROM THE DESK OF PiMP DADDY J

DATE:

SUBJECT: Jack's Lions

Ryan,
This is the drawing I was telling you about. I may not be the next Picasso but I did get creative with this one. I think its what know-it-alls like you call a metaphor. This drawing takes place in Omaha, and to be more specific, right by the Henry Doorly Zoo, where a lion escapes from its cage, moments before sharpening its teeth and scratching up the walls, chew toys, and anything else it could get its paws on. Across the parking lot of the zoo, waiting for trouble, is Thor, Hammer in hand, ready to battle. Thor gets in his battle stance preparing to take on the zoo's royalty. You'd have to be brain dead or something to think you could win in battle over this meat hungry beast. But then again, he is wearing a corn on the cob helmet, if that tells you any thing. Anyway, I hope you like it.

Sincerely,
Jared

Gay Days

In 1998, the city of Orlando, Florida voted to fly rainbow flags from its lamp posts in honor of the annual Gay Days celebration at Disney World. Pat Robertson, a well-known evangelical, and the founder of the infamous 700 Club, announced to the world that flying those rainbow flags would infuriate God, who would retaliate by destroying America by means of terrorist bombs, earthquakes, tornadoes—and if those disasters failed to do the trick, "possibly a meteor." According to Mr. Robertson, God doesn't like gays or their rainbow flags. Not one little bit.

When I first heard the reverend's statement on a radio talk show, I couldn't help but think how preposterous it sounded. *You mean to tell me that God would drop a METEOR on earth over a few rainbow flags? Rainbow flags?!?* I thought. As crazy as this idea seemed, I've always thought of myself as the sort of person who is inclined to consider the validity of any statement, no matter how improbable.

We do, after all, live on a wondrously complex and vibrant planet in the middle of an unimaginably vast galaxy, which is just one of trillions of galaxies contained in an immeasurable, ever-expanding universe, which may in fact be just one of infinite universes, hypothesized to be connected by some unseen fourth dimension. Any way you slice it—Creation or a random series of evolutionary events—we truly live in a magical place of infinite possibilities. As such, I constantly remind myself that anything, however implausible, however utterly ridiculous, could, in fact, be true.

While we're on the topic of the utterly preposterous, one of my favorite activities of all-time is to grab a glass of whiskey on the rocks, put my feet up on the coffee table in my living room or on the dashboard of my car (while it is safely parked in my drive-way), and listen intently to the claims of radical talk-radio shows.

I understood a long time ago that the people who host these programs don't necessarily believe all of the nonsense they spew over the air waves—rather, it is simply their job to spread believable bigotry. I don't say this to disparage these radio personalities. I imagine some of them are good people who love their families and their countries—it's just that they wouldn't be very good at their jobs if they weren't bigots.

In America, the only way to succeed politically is to contest your opponent at every pass; to attack every weakness, and most importantly, to make people believe that he or she is a mortal threat to whatever object or value system is in vogue at the moment: the American constitution, Judeo-Christian values, or my favorite catch-all scapegoat: FREEDOM. Oh, and calling them Hitler, fascist, socialist, and communist also works well, even if those terms represent conflicting ideologies the speaker doesn't understand.

Few things are more entertaining than listening to the far-flung conspiracy theories of these radio personalities. Unfortunately, millions of Americans take these people literally. They truly believe that our media is in cahoots with the government to bring our country to its knees, and that these few, brave journalists have exposed the painful, sobering truth. Personally, I've never had much faith in the ability of human beings to pull off intricate conspiracies. We're just too easily distracted, particularly our elected officials. You wave a few million dollars and a twenty-five-year-old with perky tits in front of a sixty-year-old bureaucrat with a leaky prostate, and there are precious few things that man won't do for you.

Pat Robertson's god, on the other hand, is supposedly immune to such temptations. Most Christians talk about the God of Abraham as if he were some perfect being, residing in a perpetual state of Zen up in his heavenly perch. Though I've never found a reason to believe in this god, I have always enjoyed imagining what he might be like.

Despite the fact that the claims of these hosts are typically outlandish at best, and that they themselves don't always believe what they are saying, that doesn't *necessarily* mean that all of their claims are untrue. I like to give people's ideas the benefit of the doubt, so when I hear a farfetched idea, I don't immediately dismiss it as a sham. I explore the idea's feasibility with a concept foreign to most political and religious commentators: objectivity.

Fortunately for me, these ideas are usually so off-the-wall that trying to logically justify them requires obscene amounts of whiskey and other mind-altering substances. In my drug-induced daydreams, God has always been a lot like me—an extremely passionate dude whose highs are only equaled by his lows. According to evangelicals like Pat Robertson, God made us in his own image. I like to imagine that he made us in his own *flawed* image.

Yep, the god I've always envisioned can go from elated to livid at the drop of the Ark of the Covenant. The day I heard Reverend Robertson's comment about Gay Days, I slipped into one of my whisky-induced day dreams, wondering: *What if this Pat Robertson character is right? What if God hates homosexuals and wants to punish all Americans with natural disasters for their sins? What if Pat Robertson really is the herald of God's wrath?*

In my daydream, I was an omniscient observer, looking down upon Disney World from a god's-eye view. On either side of the street were protesters—anti-gay demonstrators on the south side, and anti-anti-gay sign holders to the north. Those on the south side were a rag-tag bunch of Nascar-shirt-wearing country folk who looked like they had made the drive from Alabama that very morning—eleven consecutive hours in the Ford Econoline just to tell "dem queers" where to stick it. They were chanting slogans and holding protest signs. Some of their cleverer signs included:

"No Tears for Queers!"

"God Hates Fags!" I imagined an eight-year-old boy was

holding this one, clearly unaware of its message. His proud mother looked on, beaming.

"Fags Die. God Laughs." *Whoa, that's a little harsh,* I thought.

"Teabagging Our Way to Equality." Though at first it seemed these people belonged on the gay side of the demonstration, they later announced that they were from the Tea Party, and were unaware of the sexual connotation of the verb on their sign.

"Homosexuals are Gay!" *Isn't that a bit redundant?* I wondered.

On the opposite side of the street, the homosexual demonstrators, clad in Prada and rainbow colors from head-to-toe, carried signs of their own.

"No More Mr. Nice Gay." The man holding this sign was wearing a full dominatrix outfit, and he sure didn't look like a nice gay—I mean, guy.

"God Hates Your Signs!"

"If Liza Minelli Can Marry Two Gay Men, Why Can't I Marry One?" That's a fair question.

"Gay is the New Black."

And my personal favorite: "Three Words That Will Save the Economy: Gay Bridal Registry."

In my daydream, God looked down upon the demonstrators with disdain, visibly agitated by their picket signs and their rainbow flags. I imagined the archangel Gabriel at his side.

GABRIEL: My Lord, you do not look well. What is troubling you?

GOD: Those gays are at it again, Gabriel. I don't think I can take it this time. They've won over the Orlando city council, and now there are thousands of those stupid, rainbow flags flapping all over the place. I absolutely HATE those fucking flags!

GABRIEL: Yes, I see, my Lord. Forgive me for changing the subject, but we've got a serious problem.

GOD: You're goddamn right we do—those queers are waving their fruity flags all over the Florida coast. I can't look at the Atlantic seaboard without seeing rainbow colors all day long. If I wanted rainbows, don't you think I'd make it rain?

GABRIEL: I see, Lord...yes, that is troubling. Again, please forgive me for changing the subject, but I've received news that a rather powerful tsunami is rapidly approaching the coast of Indonesia. We've received half a million prayers about it in the last thirty minutes alone. If we don't act within the next hour, hundreds of thousands of people will die.

GOD: Surely you haven't forgotten that I am an all-knowing god, my dear Gabriel? I am well aware of the tsunami. If you had consulted our market penetration matrix, you would have noted that Indonesia is eighty-five percent Muslim. You honestly believe that I am interested in saving those towel-headed Allah worshippers? What's the matter, Allah doesn't answer their prayers and now they want to knock on *my* golden gates to grovel? Spare me. If I have time, I'll consider intervening, but only to demonstrate my might.

GABRIEL: But, my Lord, there are women and children—

GOD: One more outburst from you and I'll have you serving miracle duty at some back-country Baptist church on the Bayou. Now, as I was saying, I've got a gay problem in Florida. Remind me why I hired you.

GABRIEL: Yes, Lord. Have you tried using one of your messengers on earth to warn the people that the homosexuals and their flags are offensive to you?

GOD: Well, I told that idiot Pat Robertson to make an announcement on that television show of his, but he's discredited himself so much over the years that no one takes him seriously anymore.

GABRIEL: Yes, I understand—his show *is* terrible. And it doesn't help things that he looks like a pedophile. Have you considered direct intervention? I mean, couldn't you just appear to the homosexuals, tell them that their sodomy and desire for equality displease you, and command them to take down the flags?

GOD: Yes, I suppose so, but appearing to human beings is *so* Bronze Age. Besides, it's so much more fun to torment them. First, I design them to be born gay. Next, I tell them that being gay is an unnatural sin, and then I watch the psychological train wreck

93

unfold as they question their very humanity. It's the only thing that gets me through Tuesdays. I never got the hang of Tuesdays.

GABRIEL: That doesn't seem a little cruel to you, Lord? I mean, you're taking away their free will and condemning them to eternal damnation for sins they didn't willingly commit. It's like telling black people they're going to Hell for being black.

GOD: Now that you put it that way, it is a bit messed up, isn't it? Looks like ol' Lucifer rubbed off a little before I gave him the boot. *(Chuckles)*

(Enter) ASSISTANT ANGEL: Forgive me for interrupting, my Lord, but I just came to inform Gabriel that we have received another five million prayers about the tsunami since he and I last spoke, and—

GABRIEL: Right. Thank you, Louie. You may go now. Lord, now that we've only got forty-five minutes before the tsunami starts claiming its victims, isn't it about time you started inflicting your wrath on earth's homosexuals?

GOD: That's the spirit, boy—I knew you had it in you! Now, let me think...what was it that I told ol' Pat to tell the world? Oh, yes, I remember now—terrorist bombs, tornadoes, earthquakes, and... possibly a meteor. Let's start with a tornado, shall we?

Then God rolled up the camouflaged sleeves of his robe, turned his "Everything is Bigger in Heaven" baseball cap backwards, and spoke the holy incantation of queer destruction. In the blink of an eye, a massive, mile-wide tornado dropped to the ground in the middle of a farming community in central Nebraska, destroying everything in its path. Barns were leveled, cows were flung through the air, and a family of four was killed when their house collapsed upon them.

GOD: Yee haw! That'll show those homos whose boss!

GABRIEL: Pardon me, Lord, but I'm not sure how sending a tornado to the middle of Nebraska is going to send a message to homosexuals in Florida. There doesn't seem to be any correlation. You don't actually think there are any gay people in that farm town, do you?

GOD: Of course not, Gabriel. I'll just have Pat get on the television again and tell the world that the tornado was an act of retribution for the sins of America's homosexual community. How much clearer could I be?

GABRIEL: Well, Lord, you could just tell them yourself, or better yet, make homosexuality acceptable. You could do that with a wave of your hand. Besides, I'm not sure many people are going to get the connection between gays in Orlando and a tornado in Nebraska. Even with Reverend Robertson's explanation, it's a bit of a stretch.

GOD: You have absolutely no imagination, Gabriel. None.

Minutes later, Pat Robertson did as God requested and announced that the tornado in Nebraska was God's punishment for the homosexuals who had been waving their rainbow flags all over the Gay Days festivities in Orlando. While people with names like Billy Bob and Peggy Sue expressed outright disgust from their trailers in heartland of America, homosexuals everywhere went on living their lives as usual, since exactly 0.00002378 percent of gay Americans watch Pat Robertson's show. One guy in Utah is still confused.

GOD: Dammit, Gabriel, how could that plan not have worked?!

GABRIEL: Gosh, Lord, I have no idea...it was such a brilliant plan.

GOD: I know why. You were right all along—I need to be more direct.

GABRIEL: My sentiments exactly. So will you appear to the homosexuals, or just make them all straight?

GOD: Are you kidding me? It's time to unleash an earthquake of biblical proportions. But this time we will strike them in the heart: San Francisco—the epicenter of faggyness.

Gay Days

GABRIEL: What?! You do know that millions of straight people live in San Francisco, too? You'll kill heterosexuals and homosexuals alike. Plus, many of your faithful followers will perish.

GOD: Collateral damage, Gabriel. Being the chief means that sometimes you have to make tough decisions. At this point, I'd gladly sacrifice my own son to be rid of those fags and their fairy flags.

GABRIEL: But didn't you already sacrifice your...oh, never mind.

God's earthquake devastated San Francisco. The ground opened up across the city, swallowing cars whole. Buildings collapsed. The Golden Gate Bridge buckled. At least five-thousand people died. Minutes after the disaster, Pat Robertson, at God's request, informed the nation that the earthquake was God's way of punishing the city of San Francisco for its support of homosexuals. Predictably, nobody believed him. People always give God the credit when good things happen—say, a promotion, a marriage, the last slice of pie. But when disaster strikes, the blame lies with that pagan bitch, Mother Nature.

GOD: I just don't get it Gabriel. What am I doing wrong? It's not fair! I'm supposed to be infallible.

GABRIEL: God, San Francisco sits along the San Andreas fault line. It's a very earthquake-prone area. People really have absolutely no reason to believe you caused the quake.

(Enter) ASSISTANT ANGEL: I'm sorry for interrupting, but over ten million prayers have—

GOD: Gabriel, if you don't get a grip on your assistant I'm going to vaporize his eyeballs.

GABRIEL: Louie, we are aware of the tsunami and will address it at our earliest convenience. Please just set the prayer responder to "auto." Lord, I don't mean to sound repetitive, but perhaps you should consider direct contact?

GOD: You're absolutely correct, Gabriel. Let's see, we've got terrorist attack and meteor left. A meteor could mean the end of life as we know it on planet earth, so let's reserve that option as a last resort.

GABRIEL: Thank God.

GOD: You're welcome.

Soon after his discussion with Gabriel, God divinely inspired a Muslim man in Orlando to strap explosives to his chest and attempt to enter the Gay Days festivities. The man, a twenty-one-year-old student from Qatar, wore dirty Wrangler cut-off jeans, a flannel shirt, and a frayed Seattle Mariners cap as he presented his ticket at Disney World's front gate. It didn't take much more than a quick glance at the man's attire to alert the gay security guards that something was amiss. They detained him, confiscated his detonator, and called the bomb squad. The Department of Homeland Security arrested the man an hour later. As he was shipped to Guantanamo, the Gay Days attendees rejoiced in the streets. Nothing, not acts of God, not even terrorists could interfere with their festivities.

(Enter) ASSISTANT ANGEL: Excuse me, Lord, but the tsunami is less than ten minutes away from Thailand. Apparently something is wrong with the prayer relay system, because prayers from all religions are coming directly to us. We've received a hundred million prayers in the last five minutes. Something must be...

GOD: I. Told. You. NEVER. INTERRUPT. ME! RAH!!!

ASSISTANT ANGEL: Ah!! My eyes! Did you...vaporize them? Oh, the agony!

GABRIEL: My Lord...

GOD: Silence, you pacifist. Bring me Michael—I need an archangel with balls. Tell him to ready his favorite meteor. I'm a god of my word.

Soon, cries of despair filled the grounds of Disney World as men in dresses and women in ass-less chaps looked up at the sky to see their impending doom barreling down upon them. A meteor the size of Texas had completely blocked out the light of the sun as it made a beeline for the heart of Disney World.

On the other side of the planet, a tsunami brought eighty-foot waves to the coast of Thailand where hundreds of thousands met their end. Those unfortunate enough to survive were killed twenty minutes later when five-hundred-foot waves generated by the force of the meteor impact covered the entire planet with ocean water.

God looked down from Heaven with pleasure as thousands of rainbow flags disappeared beneath the salty sea. He had finally prevailed. Gabriel, the voice of reason, suggested that when God recreate the world he make it acceptable for people to be gay. As he had done to his assistant, God rewarded Gabriel for his insubordination by vaporizing his eyeballs.

Had Gabriel still possessed the capacity for sight, he might have looked down through the haze of the meteor's destruction to see me daydreaming in my car, top down, bigoted talk radio blasting. Perhaps he would see a giant parachute constructed of rainbow flags attached to my car, carrying me safely above the carnage below. He might smile at the sight of me and wonder where I was floating off to. Maybe I'd slowly drift on to the next fantasy. Only God, in his infinite wisdom, can say for sure.

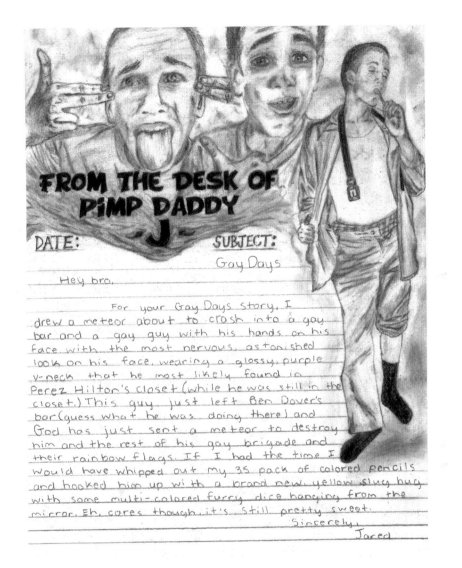

FROM THE DESK OF PIMP DADDY -J-

DATE: _____ SUBJECT: Gay Days

Hey bro,

    For your Gay Days story, I drew a meteor about to crash into a gay bar and a gay guy with his hands on his face with the most nervous, astonished look on his face, wearing a glossy, purple v-neck that he most likely found in Perez Hilton's closet (while he was still in the closet.) This guy just left Ben Dover's bar (guess what he was doing there) and God has just sent a meteor to destroy him and the rest of his gay brigade and their rainbow flags. If I had the time I would have whipped out my 35 pack of colored pencils and hooked him up with a brand new, yellow slug bug with some multi-colored furry dice hanging from the mirror. Eh, cares though, it's still pretty sweet.

                        Sincerely,
                          Jared

Caution: Bum Crossing

When I was twenty-years-old I moved into a loft in Omaha, Nebraska's Old Market district. The apartment manager was a flamboyantly gay thirty-something named Kevin who, almost immediately, developed an affinity for tormenting "the cute, straight guy," as he called me. Soon after signing the lease, I learned that I was one of only three straight tenants in the whole building and that the other two were married. Apparently, the building had an unspoken gay covenant of sorts.

At the time, I was working two jobs and carrying a full load of college classes, but Kevin didn't seem to notice or care about my responsibilities. As far as he was concerned, Tuesday was every bit as good as Saturday for an all-night rager. It was not uncommon for me to wake up in the middle of the night to Kevin and his gay entourage barging through my door, boom box blasting Madonna's "Borderline," he and his crew wearing nothing but their underwear and feather boas.

"You should be grateful, Ryan. Out of the goodness of our hearts, we were trying to include you in our Margarita Monday festivities. It's a highly exclusive club, you know. You should be honored." Kevin went on to tell me that there were dozens of pledges down at the Man Hole (his favorite gay bar) who would die to spend Margarita Monday with him. If I had any manners at all, I would have thanked him for his thoughtful intrusion.

Besides constantly invading my privacy over the two years I lived in the building, Kevin was also known for his overly-dramatic memos to the building's tenants. One winter night, after a long evening of heavy drinking with Kevin and the boys, I brought a Russian foreign-exchange student named Ivanka back to my apartment. In my lust-driven frenzy to have every item of her clothing removed by the time we reached my studio, I forgot to lock the building's security door behind us.

The first thing I realized the next morning as we made our way to breakfast, was that Ivanka's English consisted almost entirely of sexual idioms. She could tell you that she could suck a golf ball through a garden hose, but the terms *scrambled, hard-boiled,* and *over-easy* were completely foreign to her.

The second thing I noticed that morning was a memo Kevin had taped to the elevator door. It was the only note of his I ever kept, and it was also the only one that included graphic illustrations.

ATTENTION: YOU BASTARDS

How many times have I told you to close the security door to the second floor landing? How many memos do I have to write before the message penetrates your hollow skulls? Do I have to write it in blood, or would feces be a more appropriate medium, since that is what your stupidity caused me to clean up for two and a half barf-filled hours last night?

"Feces? Whatever do you mean, Kevin?" Well, since one of you is utterly incapable of performing simple motor operations within the skill set of a chimpanzee—like turning a key in a lock—a bum got into our stairwell last night and slept on the second floor landing. Actually, allow me to rephrase that. The bum couldn't have slept much, since, by my calculations, he spent at least thirty minutes grinding out a Jurassic-sized dump in front of the elevator, and at least another hour smearing it all over the walls in what looked like poopy cave paintings from a lost era long, long ago.

Have you ever seen bum poop? Never had the pleasure, you say? Don't worry, I've preserved a special sample for the idiot who left the door unlocked last night. This stuff doesn't look or smell like normal-person poop. It's other worldly. Imagine what would come out of your ass if all you consumed was colt 45 beer and leftover spaghetti from the dumpster in the alley. It's like a science experiment gone terribly, terribly wrong. Just writing about it makes me shudder.

After eight showers, I still feel as if I'll never be clean again. Thank you for showing me how rape victims feel. That's something I've always wondered about. And to think I was finally making progress with my therapist...

In an attempt to heal myself of these traumatic emotional wounds, effective immediately I am embarking on a four-day cocaine, alcohol, and sodomy binge for the record books. Regrettably, I will be unavailable to answer your requests during this time.

As we still have two more months of winter left, I would like to ask you to be more vigilant in locking the door behind you each day you come home. It's cold out there, and now that we have shown ourselves to be easy targets, the bums will no doubt try to gain entry to our building once again. Can you imagine, god forbid, if multiple bums were to get inside? I cringe at the thought of the poopy mural that would ensue.

Somewhere out there, a flea-infested bum is sitting around a garbage can fire with his homeless comrades, laughing about the huge dump and the poopy paintings he left for us. Bums are laughing at us, people. Bums. Is there really anything else to say?

Your emotionally-compromised landlord,
Kevin

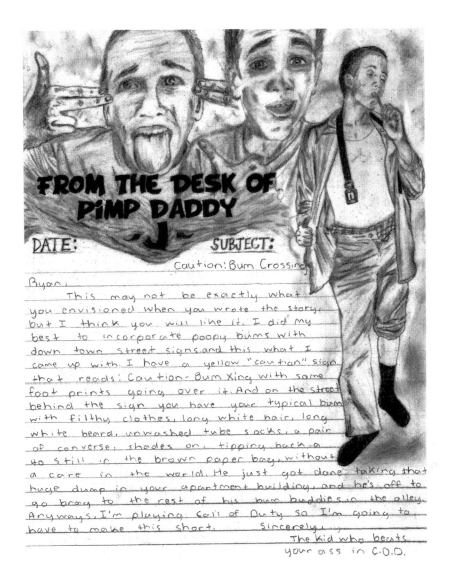

FROM THE DESK OF PiMP DADDY
~J~

DATE: SUBJECT:

Caution: Bum Crossing

Ryan,
     This may not be exactly what you envisioned when you wrote the story, but I think you will like it. I did my best to incorporate poopy bums with down town street signs. and this what I came up with. I have a yellow "caution" sign that reads: Caution-Bum Xing with some foot prints going over it. And on the street behind the sign you have your typical bum with filthy clothes, long white hair, long white beard, unwashed tube socks, a pair of converse, shades on, tipping back a 40 still in the brown paper bag, without a care in the world. He just got done taking that huge dump in your apartment building, and he's off to go brag to the rest of his bum buddies in the alley. Anyways, I'm playing Call of Duty so I'm going to have to make this short.   Sincerely,
                 The kid who beats your ass in C.O.D.

Dowry

Though at the time I had no idea the relevance foreskins played in the fable, the biblical story of David and Goliath was easily my favorite Sunday school tale. I didn't have a personal grudge against giants or anything—I suppose I just identified with David, a servant's son who rose to eternal glory. David was just an ordinary guy like me. He wasn't exceptionally big or strong, but he was brave, and he used this bravery to ascend to greatness.

I didn't necessarily want to be great, but my chubbiness and my mullet made me sort of a social outcast. It's one thing to get beat up at school, but when church kids start kicking your ass, things have gone too far. I desperately scoured the pages of David and Goliath to see if anything in the story might be able to help me change my stars.

The book of Samuel tells us that for forty days and nights, King Saul's army resisted attacking the rival Philistines, fearful of the giant Philistine champion: Goliath. Day after day, Goliath cursed the God of Abraham and dared Saul's army to cross the deep valley separating the two forces. Disgusted by the giant's blasphemy, David, who was just a teenager at the time, challenged the giant to a fight, wielding nothing more than his trusty sling.

Of course, we all know the ending to the story. David hit Goliath between the eyes with a stone, killing him instantly. He then took Goliath's sword and cut the giant's head off, casting fear into the hearts of the Philistines, who retreated back to their camp. It was a great victory for King Saul of Israel, and for circumcised Jews everywhere. No more would they have to endure jokes about their war-helmet penises. It was the Philistines, with their anteater-looking members, who should be ashamed!

Though I still had no idea what a foreskin was, for some reason I was absolutely enamored by this tale. It taught me that anyone who trusted in the Lord, no matter how small or how poor, could rise up and become great. I desperately wanted to learn more about David's life after he defeated Goliath, but our Sunday-school teacher wouldn't read the rest of the story to the class. One day, I heard the pastor talk about King David, and I wondered if he was referring to my David. Could the son of a servant eventually become the king of Israel?

Since my teacher refused to tell me the rest of the story, I decided to learn on my own. I started reading the book of Samuel where she had left off, and I soon learned that King Saul, impressed by David's victory over Goliath, promoted him to a high-ranking post in the Israelite army. In time, David became a hero of mythic proportions, reportedly slaying tens of thousands of Israel's rivals. David's military successes made Saul both envious and afraid. Paranoid that David would soon try to assume the throne, Saul plotted to kill him.

After several failed assassination attempts, Saul sent a messenger to tell David that one of Saul's daughters, Michal, loved David. Even though David could not afford a dowry, Saul would allow them to marry—on one condition—one very odd condition. Saul required that David bring him the foreskins of one hundred Philistines. I still didn't know what this curious word meant, so I naturally asked my Sunday school teacher.

The class had just dismissed, and parents were busy collecting their children from the classroom. Miss Robinson was speaking to a middle-aged woman when I interrupted. "Excuse me, Miss Robinson, I found a couple of words in the book of Samuel that I didn't understand. Could you please explain them to me?"

"Well certainly, Ryan." She replied. She was a beautiful young woman in her twenties, with big brown eyes and a Southern accent. "I'd be happy to help. What words were confusing to you?"

"Circumcision and foreskin," I stated flatly, and apparently much too loudly for her comfort.

Miss Robinson choked on the drink of water she had just taken. She looked around insecurely at the dozen or so adults in the room, who were now glaring at the two of us. "I'm, ahem, sorry...did you say...foreskin?" The second half of her sentence trailed off into a whisper. Discussing the male anatomy with a husky ten-year-old in front of a classroom full of parents was clearly outside the boundaries of her comfort zone.

"Yeah, I mean the Philistines have foreskins, but the Israelites don't. Do I have a foreskin, Miss Robinson? What about you, do you have a foreskin?"

"Well, um…well, Ryan, that is a very…uh, *delicate* subject." She scanned the angry faces of the parents in the classroom. "Actually, it would probably be inappropriate for me to discuss that with you. So, I'm going to have to ask you to not mention those words to me. *Ever.*"

I was disappointed that Miss Robinson couldn't tell me about foreskins, but it didn't stop me from reading the rest of the story. My curiosity about this mystery word was eclipsed only by my desire to learn the ending to David's story. I just told myself that foreskins were something only adults were allowed to know about, and continued reading. Saul never expected David to be able to collect the hundred foreskins—he thought that the Philistines would kill him in the process. However, David somehow success-fully completed the mission, and Saul was forced to let him marry Michal. The poor peasant was now the son-in-law of the mighty king of Israel, and would soon take the throne.

Normally I would have just moved on to the next story, but the mystery of the foreskins bothered me, and Miss Robinson's reaction only fueled my curiosity. Asking her that embarrassing question in front of the parents had apparently given me some street cred with the other students, so when they warmed up to me and told me the meaning of the word, I immediately under-stood just how odd a request Saul had made. Biblical historians tell us that Saul had no real interest in Philistine foreskins. They claim that Saul believed David would be killed during his mission, which would eliminate Saul's only real competition for the throne. But I'm not so sure. I've spent more time than I'd like to admit pondering this topic, and I have some theories of my own about what Saul really intended to do with all of those foreskins.

Genesis

KING SAUL: Servant, come here at once.

SERVANT: Yes, your highness.

KING SAUL: Look at these window treatments—aren't they the most hideous things you've ever laid your eyes upon? Just dreadful.

SERVANT: Yes. Absolutely, your majesty. Certainly not suitable for a king of your greatness.

KING SAUL: My point exactly. Now go and fetch the tailor, servant. Tell him I have a vision for my new drapes in the royal suite. I want the scene of Creation depicted in my window dress-ings. But I want it done in a mosaic style...like stained glass. Yes! That's it!

SERVANT: As you wish, your highness. And what medium should I tell the tailor to incorporate—a fine Egyptian silk, perhaps?
KING SAUL: Oh, no. I've something much finer in mind—foreskins!

SERVANT: Pardon, your highness. Did you say…foreskins?

KING SAUL (*stroking his beard and staring reverently at the sky*): Yes, Philistine foreskins—hundreds of them! And I've got just the man for the job.

The Sky Is Falling

KING SAUL (*looking out the castle window at David practicing his slingshot*): Servant boy! (*Snaps his fingers*) Get over here right now. No, closer. Come look out the window with me.

SERVANT BOY (*stuttering*): Y-Yes, your highness.

KING SAUL: You see David down there practicing his sling? Well, he has always been able to sling a stone farther than anyone in the kingdom, but lately I've noticed that he's been able to cast them extra far. I need you to befriend him and find out his secret. Can you do that for me?

(*One week later*) SERVANT BOY: Your highness, I've done as you requested. I befriended David and learned his secret, but please don't make me say it. I'm afraid you won't believe me, and you'll have me whipped for lying. It's too farfetched—it can't be true.

KING SAUL: Boy, I command you to tell me at once. I promise you will not be whipped.

Dowry

SERVANT BOY: Yes, my lord. Well, you see, after David beheaded Goliath he was still angry for the blasphemies Goliath had spoken, so he decided to circumcise the dead giant. And, well...

KING SAUL: Go on, boy. Spit it out!

SERVANT BOY: Well, your highness. As you know, Goliath was a very large man. *All* of his parts were very large. One day David was sitting under a tree, mending his sling, when he smelled the giant foreskin festering in his satchel. God came down to David and told him, "Use the Foreskin, my son." And so he did. The first stone he slung with the mended sling went further than any other he had ever cast, so he decided to make the change permanent.

KING SAUL: You mean to tell me that David used the giant's foreskin as a sling? Brilliant! He truly is God's chosen one! You've done very well, boy, but I have one final task for you. Go fetch David and the royal engineer for me. I've long wanted to build a giant slingshot to hurl boulders at the Philistines from afar, but my engineers told me that a material with sufficient elasticity did not exist. It's sort of ironic, isn't it? I mean, here we are in Israel, the circumcision capital of the world. We're waist-deep in foreskins, the very things that can help us end the war with those wrinkle-dick Philistines, and all this time we did not know the power they possessed. *(Stroking his beard and giving a sinister laugh)* Operation The Sky is Falling will move forward after all.

Dinner Guests

KING SAUL: Chef Isaac, I take it that your dinner preparations are moving ahead flawlessly, yes? The Philistine king, Abimelech, is coming for dinner, and everything must be perfect for his arrival. That bastard still has the Ark of the Covenant, and if I don't get it back, there will be hell to pay. Literally.

CHEF ISAAC: Yes, my lord. We have a fantastic seven-course meal planned for the king and his entourage. The only problem is that he requested bacon-wrapped scallops at the last minute, and well, as you know my lord, we do not serve swine in the royal dining hall. I have tried to locate some bacon for his majesty, but there is none in all of Gibeah.

KING SAUL: He requested what? I invite him into my home and he has the audacity to order pig? This is unconscionable, Isaac. I tell you, I will not stand for it!

CHEF ISAAC: So, you do not want me to prepare the bacon-wrapped scallops, my lord?

(Enter) DELIVERY BOY: I've got a priority package of foreskins for his majesty.

KING SAUL (grins and puts his arm around Isaac): Looks like bacon's back on the menu, my boy!

Capitalists

ROYAL FINANCIAL ADVISOR: Your majesty, I'm afraid I bring you grave news.

KING SAUL *(hopeful)*: David has been slain!

ROYAL FINANCIAL ADVISOR: No, your highness—goodness no! Israel's greatest hero slain? If that tragedy were to befall us, you would hear the screams of virgins committing suicide in the streets before I could ever reach these holy chambers.

KING SAUL: *(Unintelligible grunt)*

ROYAL FINANCIAL ADVISOR: Yes, as I was saying, we have a problem. You see, ever since the Philistines stole the Ark of the Covenant, commerce has diminished considerably. The twelve tribes have lost their confidence and think God has abandoned them. That downturn in tax revenue, combined with the expense of your giant foreskin slingshot, has significantly drained the royal coffers.

KING SAUL: Well, I hope you're not suggesting that construction on the foreskin slingshot be stopped. The last one to suggest that was hung with a foreskin noose. The versatility of the stuff is amazing!

ROYAL FINANCIAL ADVISOR (*nervously scratching his throat*): No, your highness. I would certainly never suggest such a thing. However, I'm telling you that if we don't do something to quickly generate revenue we'll be bankrupt by Passover. Perhaps we could sell some of those unleavened bagels with the image of the Virgin Mary on them.

KING SAUL: Don't be silly, Bobby. The Virgin Mary hasn't even been invented yet. (*Looks up to the heavens*) God, have I not been your faithful servant? Why do you surround me with these idiots? (*Looks over his shoulder at financial advisor*) Bobby, it just so happens that I commissioned the royal engineers to develop a product that might save us.

ROYAL FINANCIAL ADVISOR: That's fantastic news, your kingliness. What, may I ask, is this new product?

KING SAUL: I call it the Expanda-Bag. It starts out as just a little pouch, barely big enough to hold a single serving of matzo-balls soup. But rub the foreskin-based material, and like magic, it quadruples in size. Use it for travel, war, synagogue—the applications are endless!

ROYAL FINANCIAL ADVISOR: This is truly a brilliant idea, my king. I was hoping we could also discuss another idea—it's called credit. You see, we lend money to people in need and then charge them a fee on top of the original amount they borrowed—

KING SAUL: Yes, yes. That's all well and good, Bobby. And we may get around to it, but if we're going to pull out of this recession, we need to focus on a sure thing: the Expanda-Bag.

Bouncy Contraptions

KING SAUL: General, what is taking so long to penetrate the enemy's defenses?

GENERAL: Your highness, every time we attempt to scale their walls, the Philistines pour hot oil on our soldiers and shoot them with flaming arrows. Watching your comrades burn to death is bad for morale, and now no one will attempt to climb the walls.

KING SAUL: Yes, I see. Well, have you tried the giant foreskin slingshot? We could catapult the men over the walls.

GENERAL: We tried that, your highness, but the machine is simply too powerful. Each time we attempt to launch a man, he either flies too far and lands on the other side of the castle, or he smacks directly into the wall, dying instantly. The foreskin is powerful, but inaccurate.

KING SAUL: You dare insult the engineering marvel that is foreskin?

GENERAL: Forgive me, your highness. I meant nothing by it.

KING SAUL: Indeed. It just so happens, General, that I have a solution to your dilemma. You mock my foreskin inventions, but they will be our savior today—uh besides the Lord, our God, I mean. David, bring in your bouncy contraptions! General, I present to you the... David, what is it that you call them again?

DAVID: Trampolines, sire.

KING SAUL: Yes...trampolines. Very good.

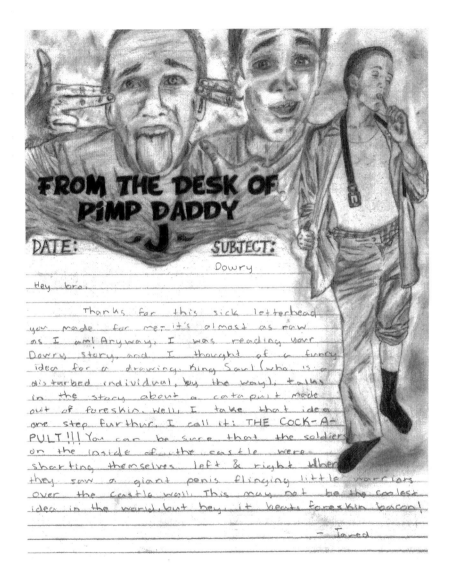

FROM THE DESK OF PIMP DADDY ~J~

DATE: _____ SUBJECT: Dowry

Hey bro,

   Thanks for this sick letterhead you made for me; it's almost as raw as I am! Anyway, I was reading your Dowry story, and I thought of a funny idea for a drawing. King Saul (who is a disturbed individual, by the way), talks in the story about a catapult made out of foreskin. Well, I take that idea one step further. I call it: THE COCK-A-PULT!!! You can be sure that the soldiers on the inside of the castle were sharting themselves left & right when they saw a giant penis flinging little warriors over the castle wall. This may not be the coolest idea in the world, but hey, it beats foreskin bacon!

                                    — Jared

My Cup Runneth Over

As I approached the Zen Meditation Center, I felt unusually anxious. After all, men have wasted away their entire lives living in isolation in caves and jungles, trying to master the precise art of meditation. I've always been a perfectionist, and though I knew that the aim of mediation was not to achieve outside recognition, I desperately wanted to be good at it. I imagined walking out of the center at the end of the day with a "Meditator of the Year" plaque, or at the very least, a certificate of outstanding meditation skills. I wondered if it was like karate class—could I earn colored belts for outstanding performance? Call it a character flaw, but I'm a competitive guy.

I learned in theology class that semester that men and women subject themselves to some of the most grueling conditions imaginable in their attempts to reach enlightenment. They believe that the essence of life is suffering, and in order to truly be happy they must become enlightened. Doing so will allow them to escape the cycle of rebirth, or *Samsara,* as it's called in ancient Sanskrit. People have been known to hold painful postures for hours, even days-on-end to catalyze enlightenment. Others have endured years of isolation in the wilderness.

These practices have always seemed counter-intuitive to me. If your objective is to permanently escape from suffering, what could possibly make you believe that subjecting yourself to unrelenting suffering is going to make you feel better? It's like telling third-world nations that the solution to their hunger is to eat less. If you ask me, I'd tell you that what Buddhists really need is to have some fun. Maybe throw back a few beers with some ladies and make some bad decisions.

This was to be my first public attempt at meditation, and despite my nervousness, I was determined to get it right. I had rented some instructional DVDs from the school library a week before, but every time I attempted to follow the instructions of the guru narrator, I ended up falling asleep and having sex dreams about my new stripper neighbor down the hall. Today, however, was a new day, so I took a determined, deep breath to boost my confidence, and walked through the front door.

When I entered the building, a short, Asian man in an orange, silk tunic silently greeted me with a welcoming smile and a bow of his balding head. He took me by the arm and showed me to my meditation pillow in the corner of the room. The meditation hall was rectangular, and contained approximately twenty small, cubby-like spaces for meditation. Each private nook boasted its own window, which overlooked the carefully-manicured garden outside. Below each window sat a miniature statue of a deity. I recognized mine, a chubby figure seated on a bag of treasure, as *Jambhuvala,* the guardian king of prosperity. He seemed jolly, unlike his ascetic counterparts; as if after having discovered buried treasure he had stumbled upon an all-you-can-eat buffet in the middle of the forest. *Some guys have all the luck,* I thought.

I sat down, "Indian style," as my kindergarten teacher used to call it, and stared blankly out the window for what seemed close to ten minutes. A dull montage of thoughts lazily passed through my mind's eye: the dirty dishes that had been sitting in my sink for the past week, the ever-elusive name of the stripper chick down the hall, the whereabouts of my lucky Frisbee—but I made an effort to ignore these distractions. Instead, I pictured the guru from the meditation tapes I had rented from the library.

"Breathe in deeply through the nose. Breathe out slowly through the mouth. You are a blank canvas. Empty your cup." That phrase—"empty your cup"—resonated with me for some reason. I took several deep breaths as the guru had instructed, and visualized myself as a cup, pouring out all of its contents.

After the third exhale, I felt something profound and completely unfamiliar happening. The sounds around me slowly faded away, and I could no longer keep my eyes open—I was slipping into an altered state of consciousness. Time stood still as I floated up a spiral passageway, toward a brilliant light source. When I reached the end of the tunnel I was engulfed by a pure, white light that filled me with a joy I had never felt before. *Is this really happening?* I thought.

Oh my god! I've read about this moment. I'm becoming enlight-ened—and on my first try! But didn't it take Buddha six years to reach enlightenment? This has got to be some kind of world record. When do I get my forty-second-degree meditation black belt? There's got to be some kind of award ceremony, right? Right?!

Soon the light faded and I began to hear voices. At first they were an unintelligible web of consonants and vowels, and for a moment I felt as if I were swimming in an audible bowl of alphabet soup. One voice soon emerged above the others, struck his gavel against an invisible sound block, and said, "Gentlemen, I would like to call to order the sixteenth meeting of the Fraternal Order of Enlightened Ones." I looked up at the speaker and saw that he was a short, Asian man with a long beard that would have given even Rapunzel beard envy. He was seated on a podium made of nebulous clouds, and as I looked down at my feet, I noticed that I, too, was sitting on clouds.

"It has been exactly three hundred and seventy two years, four months, eight days, two hours, eighteen minutes, and.... six—no, seven seconds since our last meeting," the man bellowed to the group of elderly men in attendance while carefully examin-ing his pocket watch. "I would like to thank each and every one of you for your attendance. You have been summoned here today to welcome the newest member of our order, His Holiness Ryan. Let's give him a round of applause!"

"Here, here!" The old men unenthusiastically clapped and groaned, as if the head nurse at the old-folk's home had announced it was group enema time.

I looked around the room and counted exactly fifteen men, including the man who had just spoken, seated around ornate wooden tables with lotus blossoms and misty mountains engraved upon their surfaces. The men were all very old, most of them of Asian decent, with beards that hung well past their waist lines and skin so age-spotted it looked like they had all been involved in the same devastating chemical spill. After my introduction it seemed that they had forgotten I was there. Some started conversing with old acquaintances, while others fell asleep in their chairs, creating a chorus of deep snoring.

"Excuse me," I interrupted, my voice echoing surprisingly loudly off the surrounding clouds. Several sleeping men awoke with sudden snorts of surprise, but no one responded. "Hey! Old dudes! What the hell am I doing here? What is this place?"

The man who had introduced me turned his head and responded. "I believe you already know the answer to that question, Your Holiness."

"Holiness?" I replied, annoyed. "No, I'm pretty sure I don't ask questions I already know the answer to."

"Isn't it obvious?" He asked. "You have unfilled your cup, my son."

"Unfilled my...You mean I'm...enlightened? Then that must mean that you're Buddha, right?"

"Like most things, I am nothing, but yes, there are many who call me by that name."

"I knew it!" I shrieked, unable to contain my excitement. "Booya! I did it in a day, and it took you six years of sitting under a tree. In your face, Buddha!"

"Well, that's not exactly enlightened behavior, now is it?"

"Considering that I now hold the title of fastest person to reach enlightenment, I think I'll be the judge of what is and isn't enlightened behavior."

"Touché."

"So, Buddha," I said, changing the subject. "I heard you say that this is the sixteenth meeting of the order and that you haven't had a meeting in almost four hundred years. Why is that?"

"The order convenes every time someone reaches enlightenment."

"You mean only sixteen people have *ever* become enlightened?" I asked with disbelief.

"Um..." He awkwardly stroked his beard, clearly embarrassed. "...W-We also have a female auxiliary order," he stammered. "They have twenty members. Women play a significant role in our growth plan."

"You've got to be kidding me," I griped. Though I never had much hope that Buddhism would play a major role in my life, I had always imagined that millions of Asian people and several-thousand hippies in California were reaching enlightenment all the time; their positive energy counteracting the over-indulgent, war mongering ways of the West. But these guys, they were just... pathetic. Spending eternity with them would be like a community service project that never ended.

"Well, I want out," I stated flatly. "How do I get out? Where's the exit—there's got to be a cloud staircase or a supersonic elevator or something, right?"

"What is done cannot be undone, my son. You have taken your

rightful place among the Fraternal Order of Enlightened Ones."

"What? You mean I'm stuck here? You can't be serious." I thought for a moment about my options. "I got here by emptying my cup, right? Well, I'm going to fill it back up. Watch this: I'm having impure thoughts about women. Several women. At the same time." I raised an eyebrow for effect.

Suddenly, something amazing happened. Buddha's right arm slowly became transparent, revealing the head of another guru behind him. It was working—I was filling my cup back up! I remembered stories from theology class about how enlightened masters could create hundreds of copies of themselves in their dreams and make each copy do whatever he commanded. I thought it was worth a try, so I closed my eyes and said, "I now summon my world-record enlightened powers to aid me in this time of need!"

Suddenly, dozens of beautiful, scantily-clad women appeared around the enlightened masters, three women for each old man. "Now, get me out of here!" I commanded. On my orders, the women started dancing on the tables and performing lap dances for the gurus. I looked at Buddha, who was using the only arm still visibly attached to his body to fend off a fiery redhead. I smiled at him and said, "See, Buddha, filling up your cup is fun. You should try it more often. Maybe I'll see ya in another four hundred years. Until then, keep my girls company for me."

As before, the scene faded and another white light surrounded me, this one incandescent. I awoke to the Asian man in the orange tunic gently slapping my cheek. I grabbed him by the collar, pulled his face towards mine, and blurted: "Strippers saved

129

me from Buddha!"

"Shh…you be quiet now," he scolded. He looked at the stream of drool running from my chin with unconcealable disgust. "You haf been yelling in sleep, disturbing udders' med'tayshun."

"Wha—sleep? No! I am the Supreme Enlightened One!" I declared with fleeting confidence as I looked around and noticed that nearly everyone in the hall had broken off their mediation activities to give me the classic and unmistakable "fuck you" look.

"Attention fellow meditators," I announced as I wiped the drool from my face in a series of clumsy swipes of my sleeve. "Stop what you are doing at once. It's a setup! There are only sixteen enlightened beings up there, and most of them would be banished to the nerdy table at any self-respecting nursing home. Trust me, you don't want an empty cup. Fill your cup up. Hell, let it runneth over for Buddha's sake!" I tried to summon the dancing women to help me make my case, but they were apparently indisposed.

Though it is true that I am now officially banned from both the Zen Meditation Center and the Fraternal Order of Enlightened Ones, I would be reluctant to consider this experience a failure. On the contrary, I consider my enlightenment and subsequent fall from Buddha's good graces as perhaps one of the most profound experiences of my life. I didn't even know I had a cup before. Now, as I stare at the fat Buddha statue I stole from the meditation center, I can say unequivocally that I want to fill up my cup every day of my life—maybe even overfill it once and a while. And if that means that I'm reincarnated, then so be it.

Maybe I'll come back as a jolly, fat man with a sack full of treasure and a forty-second-degree black belt, merrily whistling through the forest as he makes his way to the all-you-can-eat buffet.

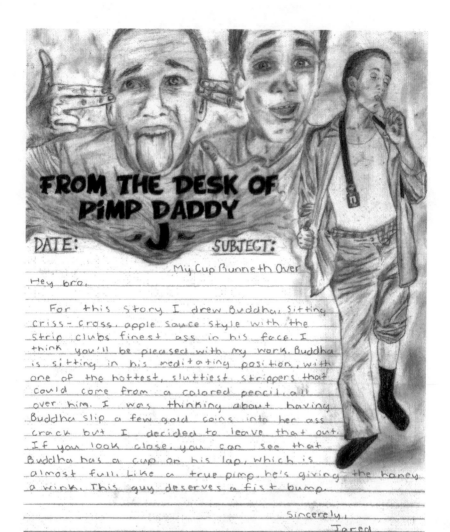

FROM THE DESK OF PiMP DADDY -J-

DATE: **SUBJECT:** My Cup Runneth Over

Hey bro,

For this story I drew Buddha, sitting criss-cross apple sauce style with the strip clubs finest ass in his face. I think you'll be pleased with my work. Buddha is sitting in his meditating position, with one of the hottest, sluttiest strippers that could come from a colored pencil, all over him. I was thinking about having Buddha slip a few gold coins into her ass crack but I decided to leave that out. If you look close, you can see that Buddha has a cup on his lap, which is almost full. Like a true pimp, he's giving the honey a wink. This guy deserves a fist bump.

Sincerely,
Jared

The Shallot

In the summer of 2009, I bought a house, got married, and was laid off from my job—all in the span of three weeks. This happened during the middle of an economic recession, and after submitting more than 150 resumes without receiving a single request for an interview, I decided to get creative. Inspired by my morning regiment of reading the satirical newspaper *The Onion* over a balanced breakfast of Fruity Pebbles and raspberry Zingers, I submitted the following story to *The Onion* in hopes that it would earn me a spot on their editorial team. After four months of silence, I assumed that my submission was somehow lost in the mail. Naturally, I sent a follow-up. Six months later: no response. My ego bruised, I vowed to found my own paper to compete with *The Onion*. I'm thinking of calling it *The Shallot,* and in classic "fuck you" fashion, the cover story of the maiden edition will feature the article *The Onion* didn't want.

Jesus Raptures Christians. Heathens Praise God, Loot Their Possessions.

WASHINGTON—In an amazing realization of biblical prophesy, Jesus Christ descended from Heaven yesterday morning to rapture millions of his devout followers. At approximately 8:42 EST, thousands of witnesses around the world reported the sound of trumpets in the sky. Shortly afterwards, dead Christians, otherwise known as the "dead in Christ," reportedly rose from their graves, floated into the sky, and disappeared.

"Yo, man. I'm tellin' ya—that was the craziest shit I eva' seen in my whole life, man," Ernest Davis, a caretaker at Blessed Orchards Cemetery told reporters shortly after witnessing the event. "I'm talkin' crazy, make-you-shit-yo'-drawers type o' shit, man. I was just sittin' there smoking a spliff, and then all of a sudden these mafuckas just started flyin' outta dey graves like some zombies 'n shit, man. That shit ain't right, yo. It just ain't right."

Seconds after the dead rose from their graves, the holy prophecy of First Thessalonians was further confirmed when Christ's living followers were also summoned to the sky. In an instant, Christians magically vanished into thin air while commuting to work, causing their unattended vehicles to careen across the lanes of the road, indiscriminately crashing into random cars, bicyclists, and buildings. Hours later, when the sun began to rise on the other side of the world, people woke up to find their spouses had simply vanished during the night.

"It was like dream come true," said Haseem Khalid Abbas, a Muslim goat herder in Syria with five Christian wives, speaking through an interpreter. "My wives always nagging me to make more money so they can buy fancy Western dresses and hip-hop albooms, but I wake up today and they all gone. Now, I claim life insurance policy on all five, get reech, and open up my very own chain of falafel restaurants. You tell me whose prayers were answered!"

The White House press secretary reported that out of the 535 members of Congress, not one individual was reported missing after the rapture. Southern Baptist deacon and Republican representative, Tom Coburn, had this to say: "There's a lot of convoluted talk 'round these parts 'bout a rapture, but I tell ya, I ain't havin' none of it. I can't tell ya if all those folks was abducted by aliens or if Mexico's simply havin' a barn burner of a sale on vacation packages, but as Jesus Christ, my lord and savior, as my witness, this ain't the rapture God talks about in the good book."

Curiously, Patricia Aguillera, a devout catholic and a White House housekeeper who had never missed a day of work in her twenty-seven years of employment, did not report to 1600 Pennsylvania Avenue for duty yesterday.

So far, public reaction to the rapture has been surprisingly positive. NFL Commissioner Paul Tagliabue, predicting improved Sunday game ratings, showed gratitude to God for the rapture. "Though I've never been a man of faith, I've got to praise God for the events of today," Tagliabue said in a press conference today. "Year after year, I've watched my hair turn gray as morning game ratings pitifully trailed behind those of the evening games. Personally, I blame it all on church. You mean to tell me that fifteen million die-hard football fans willfully *choose* not to watch Sunday's game one? No, they've been forced to miss it because their wives have dragged them to church for decades. But no more! Today is a victory for football fans everywhere."

Added Tagliabue, "On a separate note, to all the players who say prayers in the end zone after scoring a touchdown, just cut it out already. We know you're faking."

Among the many uncertainties that yesterday's epic development has generated, is the question of who is entitled to the property of these raptured individuals. In the twenty-four hours since the rapture, America has seen an unprecedented rise in squatters. Michael Savage, professor of law at Columbia University, shared his opinion about the development.

"This is the largest land-grab movement since the Homestead Act," Savage told reporters. "According to Federal law, squatters can acquire legal possession of property through a process known as adverse possession. As long as they can prove that they are improving the property in some way and that the original deed holder is aware of their presence, they can obtain legal possession of the property after the statute of limitations has expired. It's really quite ingenious if you think about it—if the original owners are in Heaven, they are obviously aware of what is happening on earth, yet ironically, they are unable to stop these squatters from seizing their property."

While the gigantic, sprawling mansions of televangelists and mega-church pastors remain occupied by their owners, millions of middle-class suburban homes across America have already started filling up with new occupants. In what has been described by the State Department as "the single greatest human migration in more than a century," hundreds of thousands of impoverished Americans from the Bayou to the Everglades have left their back-country swamps to find a better life for their families.

"Little Billy Ray ain't never seen a pool b'fore," first-time squatter Dale Tiberious Bucksley said, "but now he's gots his very own one right 'ere in our backyard. It's also the perfect habitat for his pet gator, Chicklet."

When asked if he felt his family's activities were unlawful, Bucksley replied, "Now what sort of nonsense is yew talkin' 'bout? Hell nah, it ain't unlawful. These people ain't never comin' back, so why shouldn't weeze make dere home ours? Isn't that would Jesus would want? 'Sides, this here baby's got a three car garage—big 'nuff tuh quadrupularize me moonshinin' enterprise. I don't know if God thinks he's punishin' us fer our sins, but he ain't. If this is his way of convertin' us all to worship sweet baby Jesus, it's workin'. Praise God! Hallelujah!"

As thousands of individuals like Mr. Bucksley celebrated their newly-acquired wealth, members of the Christian majority who remained after the rapture desperately scrambled to respond to claims that they were theologically-bankrupt imposters. In a last-ditch effort to turn calamity into victory, Trinity Broadcasting Network has begun an around-the-clock advertising campaign to attract the support of new constituents like Mr. Bucksley.

"What people need to understand," said long-time televangelist and TBN broadcaster Benny Hinn, "is that God left us here not because we are un-saved, but because he needs faithful servants to minister to the lost population that remains on earth. Tonight, millions of formerly-impoverished families are sleeping in new homes they have inherited from raptured Christians. Despite their sins, God has blessed them, and now he needs them to pledge their financial support to our network so that we can spread God's good word to others. Then they too can experience God's generosity. If you're hearing this message, God has called on you—he has touched your heart so that you might give. If God has given you a new home after all of your wretchedness, imagine the wealth he will bestow upon you after you start giving to the church. Come join us today so that when God returns, you'll be ready to join him in paradise."

Trinity Broadcasting Network stock rose today by thirty-seven percent, the largest single-day rise in the network's history. Though we have yet to see the prophesized rise of Satan in this post-rapture world, one thing is certain: it will take more than the rapture of every Christian on the planet to stop the juggernaut that is Christianity.

Reverend Rob
& The Baloney Bopper

"Sorry for droppin' in on ya unannounced and all, Rye. I didn't catch ya boppin' yer baloney did I?" Barely two months had passed since my wife and I had moved out of Rob's neighborhood and into our new house three miles down the road. The dozen or so times he had stopped by, this was invariably his greeting of choice. He would pull up ten in the morning, slam the door of his rusty Ford pickup truck, and knock on my door. When I answered, he would inquire as to whether his visit had interrupted the slaughter of millions of defenseless sperm, and then offer me a cold beer. He performed these actions in exactly this order every visit, as if reading from a script.

Had I not, in fact, been giving my baloney a proper bopping one of the first times Rob dropped in unannounced, his teasing wouldn't have bothered me. I would have passed it off as just another example of his less-than-conventional methods of masculine communication. Some people apologize for calling during dinner. Rob expresses his regret for having interrupted what he assumes was your meeting with the one-eyed yogurt thrower.

But even though I was certain that Rob hadn't actually seen me punching my munchkin at my new house, his remark bothered me. Not only the presumptuous nature of the statement, but also the nonchalant way in which he delivered it. The casual tone he employed is typically reserved for sports chit-chat—as in, "I hope I didn't interrupt your Super Bowl party." If Rob truly wanted to tease me about doing the knuckle shuffle on my piss pump, he would have given me a much harder time. Instead, his statement came across as almost confessional, and I began to wonder if at one point while sneaking around our old neighborhood (which he often did), he had caught me in the act. Soon I found myself checking around corners and rapidly whipping up window curtains, confident I would find him lurking there. I haven't been able to comfortably fondle my fajita since.

My suspicion stemmed from two events. The first was something Rob said to me on my wedding day. The second had to do with the circumstances surrounding my first encounter with Rob. Several years earlier, my fiancée and I had rented a house across from Rob and his wife. The brick home was located in a quiet Denver suburb with wide streets, mature trees, and expansive backyards—perfect for dog lovers like us. It was the end of our first week in the neighborhood, and I had just returned home from a typical day of medieval torture at the office. I turned the key in the front door and braced myself for the usual, saliva-filled greeting I had received every day since adopting our mixed breed dogs from the shelter. This day, however, the dogs did not meet me at the front door. I walked through the house to the sliding glass door that led to the back yard, and found them nuzzling with a strange man in the grass. Instinctively, I opened the door and shouted at him.

"What in the hell do you think you're doing in my back yard?" I demanded. "Get away from my dogs!" I commanded the dogs to come to me, but they refused to leave the man's side, their tails excitedly whizzing from side-to-side.

"Now, just calm down there, bud," the man calmly replied after what looked like a painful, yet satisfying swig of beer. He stood up, and I noticed that he was tall, maybe six-feet, with a slightly muscular build that suggested he knew his way around a construction site. And he was older, probably in his late fifties, with a wiry, unkempt beard that moved like a fuzzy marionette when he spoke. "It's all cool and the gang, bud," he assured me. "I'm Robert—Robert Anderson. I'm your neighbor. I live just across the street." He motioned over my shoulder, a mostly smoked and entirely forgotten nub of a cigarette perched between his broad fingers. "I take care of things around here."

"What do you mean you *take care of things* around here?" I demanded. "Are you the maintenance guy or something? You can't just come over unannounced, you know."

"Nah, I just take care of things around the neighborhood," he replied, stoically staring off into the distance. "Keep an eye out, if you know what I mean." It was more a statement than a question, and as counterintuitive as it was, I felt I did know what he meant. "I saw the electric company inspecting the transformer back here, and I wanted to make sure those cocksucking thieves didn't mess around with your meter while they were at it. Those pricks are always trying to roll our meters forward whenever they come out."

He took another deep gulp of beer. It bothered me how comfortable he was. He was trespassing on private property, yet he might as well have been in a terrycloth robe at a four-star hotel. As crude as he came across, there was an air of sophistication about him. The way he carried himself; the slow, methodical manner in which he spoke, his silent confidence—it was almost genteel.

"But don't worry about that meter," he continued. "I went ahead and rolled that sumbitch back for ya. It'll be like a free month of electricity for you and the little lady, so crank up that AC, brother." He smiled so joyfully at the thought of stealing power from the utility company that his eyes actually closed for a moment, sending a network of deep lines racing across his brow. He then reached into his back pocket and pulled out a bottle of beer. "Care for a cold one?"

When he extended his hand to pass me the bottle I noticed that the nail on the index finger of his left hand had grown into a painful-looking, convex arch. It was the kind of injury that could only have resulted from a full-on strike from a carpenter's hammer. I stared at the gruesome nail in a momentary daze. I had barely spent two minutes with Rob, but he was more interesting to me than anyone I had met in years. Like a botanist who discovers a new species in the rain forest, I resolved to intensely study my subject. I enthusiastically snatched the bottle from Rob's hand, popped the top, and chugged what was to be the first of many cold beers we would share.

In the weeks that followed our first encounter, I learned that Rob did in fact "take care of things" around the neighborhood. On any given weekend he might take four hours to make his rounds: stopping at Jerry's to help harvest tomatoes from his garden, helping Helen move boulders into her back yard, or just talking shop with Dave, the sheriff, who lived directly across the street from me.

"I don't mean no disrespect," he told me one afternoon, "but I saw Dave and his cop buddies practicing their Tae Kwon doo nonsense yesterday on the front lawn." Rob often began sentences in this way. He would say he didn't mean any disrespect and then immediately proceed to utter a disrespectful remark.

"Those goddamn pussies better not try any of that dancin' ninja bullshit on me, or I'll shove my fist so far up their corn holes they won't be able to have any of their homo butt-sex for months. Tae Kwon doo not fuck with this white boy." The rant seemed light-years out of place coming from a man who would soon be collecting social security.

Most people would have dismissed Rob's tough talk as harmless—nothing more than the ramblings of an aging man who needed to reassure himself that he had once been a young, good-looking lady's man, running wild in the world's greatest city. But when I looked into his eyes, I felt that Rob sincerely believed that he could still handle himself. And about two months after we moved in, I witnessed him prove it.

Around seven o'clock one evening, I happened to look out my window and notice a brown, rusty Chevy Caprice Classic parked in front of Rob's house. The driver and passenger were both in their early twenties, and they sat in the car for over thirty minutes, talking on their cell phones and periodically taking pictures of Rob's and his neighbor's houses. It seemed like suspicious behavior, so I called Rob on his cell phone to let him know what was happening. He responded that he was five minutes away, but would be home in two. No matter where you were in town, Rob always seemed to be five minutes away.

In typical fashion, I heard Rob before I saw him. He had a deep, grizzly voice like work boots on gravel, so understanding him from a distance was often a problem, particularly if he was yelling. And you can bet your ass he was screaming this day. I couldn't make out every word from my living room, but when I heard "gun," and "skull fuck your eye sockets" in the same sentence, I decided to go outside and try to mediate the situation. When I arrived on the scene, I found Rob in the middle of the street, screaming and wildly waving a black pistol at a car whose driver was now desperately trying to put as much distance as possible between himself and Rob's skull-fucking hand cannon.

Rob received a letter from Google the following week, informing him that the individuals in the car were taking photos of houses on the block for inclusion in the company's online street-view project. "How in fuck's name was I supposed to know they were from the Googler?" he grunted. "For all I know they could have been from the IRS. Honestly speakin', my taxes ain't exactly legit, if you know what I'm sayin'."

Despite my every instinct telling me to keep my distance, Fate made sure that Rob and I spent a great deal of time together in the months following the Google incident. My fiancée traveled two weeks each month for work, so I tackled a number of home improvement projects to keep myself occupied while she was away. Rob felt it was his neighborly duty to keep me company while she was gone, and he often helped me with my projects. I eventually borrowed so many tools from him that he ended up just giving me the key to his tool shed. And though part of me suspected that if I ever crossed him he would call the cops and make it look like I was stealing his tools, I knew the gesture meant that he considered me his friend.

Soon, Rob and his wife started regularly inviting me over for dinner. After a few whiskeys too many, Rob would open up to me about his past. He particularly enjoyed telling me about his father, who according to him was at one time a successful movie and television producer in New York City. It soon became clear to me that Rob's father was the only person he had ever admired. But he didn't look up to him because of his professional accomplish-ments, which included working on several Hollywood motion pictures. Rob admired his dad for the way he carried himself. He would often talk about his father as if he were a mafia don—a man who commanded respect and admiration wherever he went. Rob's father always had a fat wad of hundred-dollar bills in his pocket, and plenty of swooning ladies to help him spend it.

"But he always got those FICO scores, Rye Rye," Rob would say. "If my daddy taught me anything it's that you never marry a broad with bad credit. You gotta tell them bitches to give you them scores, or get the fuck out." Rob made the strategy sound pretty straight forward, but when I asked my fiancée for her credit scores, all I got was the bedroom door slammed in my face.

Rob's father endowed him with a wealth of guidance pertaining to the opposite sex. This advice revolved around a grade-school-style ranking system. You started at kindergarten, and as your knowledge of women increased, so did your corresponding grade. "For example," Rob told me, "second grade is the ice-cube test. Let's say you sit down to lunch with a woman and the waiter brings out your glasses of water. If those glasses contain ice-cubes and your little lady doesn't blush, then your ass hasn't mastered the secrets of grade two. Your dumb ass flunks and has to start over." It was the sexual equivalent of Boy Scouts, except instead of patches you earned your manhood. Rob refused to tell me the secrets of the grading system, and to this day I remain uninitiated. All I know is that grade four has to do with chinchillas and anal intercourse. According to Rob, I don't have the stomach for it.

Rob's father also advocated a strict "no glove, no love" policy. "My father always used to tell me," Rob once said, "Son, I don't care if you bang up all the little girls on the block—just don't knock any of 'em up, and it's cool and the gang. But if your ass brings home a little bastard baby to my doorstep, I'll forget I ever knew you."

But the Anderson philosophy wasn't just some misogynistic anthem of carnal irresponsibility. Both Rob and his father had a deep appreciation for women and for their wives, who they respected and loved deeply.

"It's like this," Rob would say. "After a long night of bangin' a smokin' hot chick, you typically wake up the next morning, and that broad is stupider than a night clerk at a Motel Eight. You've got nothin' to talk about with these kinds of chicks, and while they're great for bangin', they're not good for much else. That's about eighty, maybe ninety percent of most of the women out there." He stopped for a moment to scratch his head and re-calculate his math. Once he was certain about the percentages, he went on.

"But every once in a while, you'll find that rare woman who'll wake up next to you, make a joke about your pecker, and start cooking you an omelet. Conversation will be easy with her, but you won't always feel the need to speak. She may not be the one you're going to marry, but then again, you never know. You may only meet a couple of women like this in your whole life, so you've got to be careful that you treat these ones right. Because in the end, after you're too old to bang all the young little honeys on the block—and I'm not saying that I am..." He paused long enough to make certain I was fully aware that he could still satisfy a young woman. "...Anyway, all I'm sayin' is that a man is only as good as the woman by his side."

Credit scores and pregnancy aside, Rob's father passed down few other rules regarding women. But there was one rule that was to be respected above all others. Never, under any circumstance, was it acceptable to lay a hand on a woman. To do so was to violate the most sacred and primordial code of manhood. The punishment for this indiscretion was banishment from your core circle of friends and family, and quite possibly, intense physical pain by Rob's hand. As Rob would say, "We've got to protect the women folk."

I found out about this rule the hard way. My wife and I were a newly-engaged couple in our twenties. Not having sex for the two consecutive weeks when she traveled for work was nearly unbearable. When she returned after a long trip she didn't have time to set down her suitcase before I hurled her over my shoulder, Tarzan style, and carried her to the bedroom. She has always been one of the more—ahem—sexually vocal women I have ever been with, but she was especially loud on days when she returned home from a trip. After a particularly raucous episode, I left the house to pick up some Chinese take out. When I returned home I noticed Rob leaving our house.

"Hey, buddy!" I shouted after him. "Shoot anybody from the Googler lately?" But he just glared at me and walked away.

When I got inside the house, my fiancée informed me that Rob had stopped by to let her know that all she had to do was say the word and he would take a baseball bat to my knee caps.

"He thinks I'm beating you?" I asked in disbelief. "Why didn't you just tell him we were having sex?" I demanded, careful to keep my voice down so that Rob couldn't hear us from across the street. I went to the front door and carefully peeked out the window to make sure he wasn't prowling about nearby.

"I don't know!" she shot back. "What was I supposed to do? Tell him that my screams of ecstasy sound like the cries of a battered woman? I just couldn't do it."

"Well, that's just great," I replied. "Instead, you let an armed, murderous lunatic with a complete disregard for authority—and more importantly, our private property—think that I'm beating you. Great plan. Did you take out another life insurance policy on me or something?"

Rob kept his distance for the next few months. Occasionally, I would come home to find him greeting our dogs through a small hole in the front gate, but upon seeing me he would immediately dust the dog treat crumbs from his hands and leave. He'd mumble something to me as he left like, "I was just sayin' hi to the peanuts."

Peanut was his universal name for dogs. Sometimes, when referring to a dog that wasn't present, he'd use the dog's name, followed by the word "dog," which functioned something like a last name. As in, "I just stopped by to give the Bailey Dog his bone." Other words for dog included fuck head, fucker, little fucker, and doodle. But peanut was the most commonly-used form, and my favorite.

Though Rob's menacing silent treatment made me constantly fear for my physical welfare, it turned out to be well-timed. My fiancée and I were just four months away from our wedding date, and still had a long list of wedding tasks to complete. Flowers had to be ordered. Bridesmaid gowns needed selecting. But the most elusive undertaking of the entire planning process was selecting the person to perform the ceremony. My former boss at the Environmental Protection Agency was our first choice, but since he was a Catholic Deacon, he could only perform the service if we converted to Catholicism. This process involved getting baptized and paying for a series of marriage counseling courses. For us, this meant that our wedding would have directly funded the sodomy of choir boys. I'm as socially apathetic as the next guy, but I just wasn't OK with the idea.

In the state of Colorado, anyone can perform a wedding ceremony. A simple Google search—while discouraged by Rob—produces a variety of outlandish characters that provide an added flair to Denver weddings. There's Willy the Wedding Wacko, a fire-juggling clown who escorts the bride down the aisle on his unicycle. For a suggested donation of sixty-six chicken hearts, Calypso Karen performs a voodoo ceremony whereby each party is obligated under punishment of death to remain faithful to one another. *His and hers voodoo dolls sold separately.* A comedian who goes simply by the name "Bob" offers his comedic wedding services via Craigslist ads. His fee is two hundred and fifty dollars. His accepted method of payment? Cash, check, or scotch.

Each whack job was worse than the next, and with our wedding coming up in less than 60 days, we were becoming desperate. Normally we would have done what we usually did when we had a problem: have an earsplitting session of spearing the bearded clam. It's a therapeutic process I like to call bang storming. But since the incident with Rob, we were trying to be more discreet.

Convinced that our sexual frustration was at the heart of the problem, I devised a plan. It took me a few days to write the script, and to time the performance so that Rob would hear it, but we finally decided upon a Saturday afternoon when Rob and his wife were guaranteed to be home. I anticipated that even with Rob's keen sense of hearing and his penchant for being in the know, he would have missed some of the first lines of our play. That's why

I placed the juiciest lines in Act II.

HER: "Oh, Ryan, I love it when you put your ENORMOUS penis inside of me when we have really, really loud sex that—OOOhh-hhhhhh—sounds like domestic violence, but is really just mind blowing, earth shattering, SEX!!!"

ME: "Oh yeah! It feels so good to have SEXUAL INTERCOURSE with you. In case anyone is listening, there is absolutely no domestic violence happening right now—not even a playful spank on the butt. Just me using my GIGANTIC PENIS to have SEXUAL INTERCOURSE with my fiancée in our domestic-violence-free household."

I drove my fiancée to the airport the next morning, and it may have been my imagination, but it seemed to me that there was an unusual amount of neighbor ladies gardening in spandex pants in their front yards.

When I returned home two hours later, I found Rob waiting for me on my doorstep. In customary fashion, he pulled a beer from his overalls, gestured for me to sit down next to him, and passed me the bottle. No matter the time of day, I never refused a beer from Rob. It was something you just didn't do, like pass on a cigar from a mafia don.

I waited for him to say the first word. His eyes fluttered about my front yard, never focusing on any single item for more than a split second. He took successive drags from his cigarette, as if the next words he would speak were hidden somewhere deep in the smoke.

"Listen, dude," he began abruptly. "You may never hear me say this again, so listen up and relish this moment if you're in to that sort of thing." He paused again, his eyes darting about like how people's eyes move when they're having a really intense dream. Then, with a heavy sigh that dropped from his mouth like a bag of burlap, he uttered something I never imagined I would hear him say to me.

"I apologize." I waited for him to go on, but he just sat there, squeamishly staring about, clearly experiencing a momentary identity crisis. He was the captain and I was his first mate. The whole goddamn world was his crew. He didn't apologize to his subordinates. Rob's ship was capsizing and he didn't know how to right her.

"Yeah, I guess I kinda fucked up," he somberly continued as if confessing to a priest. "Truth be told, I didn't think you were capable of laying the pipe like that, dog. I thought for sure you were beatin' her. You know I love that little lady, and there was no way I was gonna let that slide. But I want you to know that even though I've been acting like an asshole towards you for the past couple of months, it's only 'cuz I love the shit outta you guys and want what's best for ya. Me and my old lady, we could never have kids—not because of my sperm, obviously, 'cuz you know they're the bomb—and since you two moved in we sorta started looking at you in that way."

It was Rob at his most vulnerable, and though I was relieved

153

to hear my acquittal from the mouth of my accuser, Rob's reaction made me uncomfortable. Something told me that I couldn't leave him alone like that. I spent that entire Sunday with Rob, drinking whiskey well into the evening. He told me all about his father's career in cinema and his time hanging out with the Black Panthers in Brooklyn. He even painted a little in his thirties—but only oils. He wouldn't admit it in front of his wife's artist friends, but Rob thought acrylics were for pussies.

As I fought off a belly laugh from one of his painting jokes, I received a call from my fiancée. I told her that Rob and I had reconciled, and that I had an idea I needed to share with her. I had a half-bottle of whiskey splashing around in my belly, so I needed her approval before I moved forward with my plan. After I explained it to her, she eagerly agreed, so I hung up and told Rob I had to run home for a few minutes.

"Shuure, bud. I gets it," he slurred. You gots 'ta get a lil' bit uh that phone-sexy time in. No worriez, boss. That little honey of yours gots an insasheaable appertite on her, anz you're the main course. Jus' do me uh faver 'n stay away from the poo poo platter."

I returned to Rob's backyard ten minutes later, holding a piece of paper. I casually set it down beside him and waited for him to pick it up.

The paper read:

CREDENTIALS OF MINISTRY

THIS IS TO CERTIFY THAT THE BEARER HEAROF:

Robert Paul Anderson

HAS BEEN ORDAINED THIS 21ST DAY OF MAY

AND HAS ALL RIGHTS AND PRIVILEGES TO

PERFORM ALL DUTIES OF THE MINISTRY

"So what do you think, bud?" I asked. "You think you're up to the task? We're in desperate need of a minister and seeing as how I just ordained you online, you're now fully qualified. Would you do us the honor?"

It was the first time I saw Rob cry.

The second and last time I saw Rob shed a tear was the day of our wedding. He donned a maroon and white ceremonial priest's garb, which he proudly claimed to have stolen from a church while re-wiring their stage lights. On his feet he wore a pair of red, patent leather Air Jordan sneakers. I never asked him what his obsession was with those shoes, but they were truly hideous. His usually untidy hair and beard were neatly combed. In his right hand he held a bottle of Bud Light and in his left, a flaming Marlboro Red. Wedged under his arm was a crinkled stack of pages containing the full text of the service he had prepared.

Soon the sun descended toward the horizon, casting a golden glow on the foothills to the north. The bridesmaids and grooms-men took their places on either side of the iron archway where we were to be married. A mother goose ushered her newborn goslings to the other side of the adjacent pond, safe from our curious, mud-covered dogs. Across the meadow, a hungry horse impatiently grunted at a ranch hand, inquiring about the evening hay.

Rob's service was profound and beautiful, like something out of a movie or a romance novel. He effortlessly moved from Shakespeare to Rilke to Rumi, but in classic Rob style, his man-nerly conduct soon yielded to his inner electrician. At one point he forced himself to stop in order to fight back his tears, explaining that he was sorry, but he just "loves the shit out of these guys."

Some people laughed. Others cried. When he finally pro-nounced us husband and wife, I kissed my bride and the crowd cheered. Rob shook my hand and whispered in my ear. "Even if you do play with yourself too much, I still think of you as a son."

But before I made the connection, he went on, "Now go take that bride of yours back to that cabin and show her what kind of a man she just married. You make her scream so loud that she scares away all the wildlife for a ten mile radius. Then maybe, just maybe, we'll talk about graduatin' ya from ol' Reverend Rob's school of mackin' broads."

I smiled and turned away, but he called after me. "Hey, bud—one last thing. What'd your old lady think about those pre-nuptial clauses we came up with the other night? Did you get her to sign?" I shook my head and laughed, as if to say he were crazy.

He dropped his cigarette on the ground and snuffed it out with his ridiculous shoes. In one gulp, he finished the rest of his half-full beer.

"Goddamn rookie," he muttered, and walked toward the outhouse to take a piss.

FROM THE DESK OF PIMP DADDY ~J~

DATE: **SUBJECT:** Reverend Bob

Ryan,

    Here's the picture of the priest I was telling you about. Not some of my best work but I think you will like it. When you first asked me to draw this picture I took out my notebook and began to experiment. When I started drawing this I tried thinking back to your wedding, but all I could remember was Bob leaning against an old, wooden Porta-Potty with 2 cigs in his mouth and a beer in his hand, like he was in a Grease movie or something. He was talking to some old dude who was waiting to take a leak. The thing about that conversation that made it stick to my brain was the fact that he ended it saying... "Well, gotta go. I saw some hotty teenager shaking her ass on the dance floor, and I think it's time to go slip some vodka into her Kool-Aid. The look on that old guys face said it all.   Sincerly,

                          Jared

Failed Prenuptial Clauses

Doesn't every man wish he could somehow coerce his bride-to-be into signing a one-sided prenuptial agreement? Well, I've always fantasized about it, and my priest, Reverend Rob, helped me realize that dream. Here are some of the clauses that failed to make the cut.

Girly Movies

COUPLE agrees to maintain a household free of gratuitously girly movies. Upon execution of this agreement, WIFE hereby agrees to hold HUSBAND faultless for burning titles such as THE TWILIGHT SAGA (or any other movie with an absurd plot involving vampire/werewolf/human love triangles), LEGALLY

BLONDE, THE PRINCESS DIARIES (2 DISC COLLECTORS SET), MEAN GIRLS, WHAT A GIRL WANTS, BRING IT ON, and BRING IT ON AGAIN. Any movie falling under this genre is subject to burning and/or smashing at any time.

Ethnic Twins

If at any juncture in the relationship, COUPLE is approached by female twins of any nationality who are willing to engage in sexual activity with COUPLE, WIFE is hereby obligated to engage in said acts, and to admit to friends and acquaintances that said acts took place. If COUPLE has access to a video recorder at the time of sexual acts, video documentation shall be obtained. In the event of dissolution of marriage, HUSBAND reserves the right to publish video evidence of sexual acts on the internet. If said internet leaking results in a lucrative acting career for WIFE, as is the trend in Hollywood these days, HUSBAND shall be entitled to half of all net proceeds of WIFE's Hollywood earnings.

Lottery Winnings

In the event HUSBAND wins a lottery jackpot in an amount exceeding one million U.S. dollars ($1,000,000), he shall be entitled to take a sabbatical by himself, or with the company of his friends, not to exceed thirty calendar days, during which time any and all actions performed by HUSBAND, in violation of this agreement or any applicable state or federal laws or otherwise, shall not entitle WIFE to any legal means of recourse whatsoever. Examples of acceptable behavior include throwing lavish parties in five-star, Las Vegas hotel suites with an entourage of professional escorts, skydiving naked, chartering a private flight to the International Space Station, and any other immediately gratifying carnal pleasure of HUSBAND's choosing.

At the conclusion of the sabbatical, any remaining lottery winnings must be equally divided between HUSBAND and WIFE. This clause is valid for scratch, pull, and draw tickets, as well as Keno, horse racing, sports betting, lottery machines, and table stakes gambling. Should WIFE win the lottery, all of her winnings shall be equally divided between COUPLE. She shall not be entitled to a sabbatical of any sort, though she is allowed to go to the dollar theatre to see any film, provided she goes alone.

Weight Gain
WIFE must maintain, except during times of pregnancy, a weight between 120 and 127 pounds, as measured by a standard, medical-grade scale for which she is solely responsible for the purchase and maintenance. After delivering a newborn child, WIFE has no more than seven weeks to return to this weight range. Otherwise, any infidelities by HUSBAND shall be nullified.

Celebrity Sexual Advances
In the event that HUSBAND has the opportunity to obtain carnal knowledge of an A, B, or C-list celebrity, he may do so freely.

WIFE may not use acts as grounds for divorce or for seizure of assets. D-list celebrities from reality shows such as *The Real World, Jersey Shore, Rock of Love,* and especially, *Sarah Palin's Alaska,* are excluded. WIFE may also obtain carnal knowledge of celebrities; however, her choices are limited to Chuck Norris, Steven Seagall, Chuck "The Iceman" Liddell, Lou Ferrigno, Sean Connery, Jack Nicholson, and Dustin Hoffman, provided he maintains the *Rainman* character throughout said sexual acts.

Fat Jeans

Should WIFE ask HUSBAND if a pair of jeans makes her butt look fat, HUSBAND shall not be held liable for honesty. Answers such as, "No, honey, it's your butt, not your jeans, that makes your butt look fat," are acceptable. Refer to the "Weight Gain" clause of this agreement for rules concerning WIFE's acceptable weight range.

Crying for no Reason

Under no circumstances shall WIFE cry without justification. When asked what is wrong, WIFE shall not sobbingly answer "I don't know." Violations of this clause will result in a $1,000 fine or 10 blowjobs (hereinafter, ORAL COMPENSATION), or the equivalent fair market value ratio of dollars to ORAL COMPENSATION. Monetary and ORAL COMPENSATION cannot be combined. Acceptable reasons for crying include, loss of limb (excluding fingers and toes), the Nebraska Cornhuskers losing the Big 12 Championship, and the death of any Saturday Night Live cast member (excluding Ellen Cleghorne, Chris Kattan, and Victoria Jackson.)

Padded Toilet Seats

Under no circumstances shall WIFE install padded toilet seats in COUPLE's home. HUSBAND is simply freaked out by them.

Public Service Announcement

When you plan your wedding you have no idea what a sadistic ambush you are preparing for yourself. Despite years of experience and your common sense telling you otherwise, you imagine that your unruly family and friends will somehow, overnight, garner the self-restraint to set aside all of their petty bickering, unnerving habits, and self-centeredness, and out of respect for the sacredness of your upcoming union, refrain from behaving like escapees from a maximum security asylum. At the very least you hope that they do not treat your wedding as an audition for a reality TV show.

Maybe this is a naïve desire. Perhaps expecting an eclectic gathering of one hundred random strangers to do anything other than be on their absolute worst behavior is unrealistic. After all, you are supplying them with free food, enough booze to inebriate a third-world nation, the spectacle of true love, and afterwards, you encourage them to party all night. To any rational mind this sounds like a recipe for disaster—or a frat party. But with a divorce rate above fifty percent, two people who choose to get married in this day and age are anything but rational.

My wedding was so—ahem—eventful that I decided to create a series of public service announcements for future newlyweds. If these announcements somehow accidentally slip into your guests' invitations, then maybe, just maybe they will behave like responsible adults. But I'd suggest having the fire department on stand-by just in case things get out-of-hand.

Ring Toss

I know. Really, I do. You're on vacation in a beautiful setting. You just witnessed a lovely wedding ceremony, and now you're enjoying a delicious meal under the twilight. Your third glass of wine sends a warm, pleasant sensation through your entire body. The cool mountain breeze is brisk and invigorating. If only your fiancée would look into your eyes and tell you how much he loves you, this moment would truly be perfect. Unfortunately, he's already drunk and is talking loudly to another girl across the tent.

Understandably, your first reaction might be anger, but please resist the urge. You are going to be married soon yourself, and that means you trust your partner, right? Don't you want your soon-to-be husband to meet the family of your cousin's new wife? After all, soon they're going to be his family as well.

Good, he's coming back. Now's the time to tell him how

deeply you care for him, how glad you are that you took this trip together, and how much you are looking forward to spending the rest of your life with him. Now is definitely not the time to take off your engagement ring, throw it in his face, and shout that you hope he's happy with that slut (who just happens to be the bride's sister). Nope. It's definitely not the time for that.

GPS

If you're the disc jockey for a wedding in the middle of a national forest, it's probably a good idea to drive by the grounds before the day of the wedding just to be sure you know where you're going. Whatever you do, do not rely on your GPS device to get you there, get lost on the way, and then arrive two hours late to the ceremony.

I'm no GPS expert, but I'm fairly certain that the GPS people don't have every forest in North America uploaded into their computers. Besides, no one is going to wait around for two hours just so you can play one song for the bride to walk down the aisle. The crowd will probably just break out into a rendition of "You've Lost That Love and Feeling" and get on with it.

Oh, and when you do finally arrive, an hour into the reception, don't make excuses. It's not your GPS's fault that you're a douchebag. No, giving a fifty dollar discount will not make a difference. Everyone will still think you suck. And they'll be right.

Best Man

You're going through some tough times with the wife, and you've begun to ask yourself if she's truly the one for you. You've thought about leaving her, but things are complicated. You've got kids together, a house—goldfish even. But you've decided you're going to put all of that aside for the weekend. Despite the things you've said and done over the years, you've been asked to be the best man of your buddy's wedding. You guys aren't as close as you once were, but you've been friends for most of your lives and you really want to restore that bond. This weekend could take your friendship a huge step in the right direction.

You've tried to tell yourself that this weekend is about your friend, but everything your wife does just bugs the hell out of you. She's letting the kids run wild all over the place, she's drinking too much, and she wore a white dress to the wedding. Who does that? You've successfully looked past all of these indiscretions, and it seems like you and your buddy are getting things back on track. But then you look across the reception hall and see her posing for a picture with a guy you've never met. *What in the hell is his arm doing wrapped around her?*

Whatever you do, do NOT march across the room, call her a whore, push him in the chest, and start a fist fight in the middle of the reception. Your wife is going to think you're a jealous jerk, and you're probably going to get demoted from your best man status.

Yep, you definitely just got demoted.

Belts

Belts are these amazing contraptions that hold your pants up. When you are selected to be a groomsman, it's a good idea to wear a belt. If you don't, you'll forever be thought of as that guy who ruined all of the wedding photos because he didn't have a belt on. No, un-tucking your shirt to cover up your belt-lessness will not help.

That Guy

Getting drunk before a coworker's wedding is never a good idea. You might think to yourself that having a few mixed drinks at a summertime barbeque is going to get you primed for the wedding, but drinking in the daytime in general is usually ill-advised.

Yes, there are always a few people at every wedding who get absolutely hammered. This is inevitable, and in some ways, expected. However, this privilege is usually reserved for parents, surrogates, and life-long friends. If you do not fall into one of these categories, you can't get fall-down drunk. I'm sorry. Life is unfair.

If you find yourself in a situation where you are clearly too drunk to drive home, the hosts will feel obligated to put you up for the night. Make no mistake—they are annoyed by you and would rather you weren't there. In fact, they probably only invited you because inviting some coworkers and not others is considered rude. They'd just rather not have you crash into a pine tree on your way home and have the memory of their wedding tarnished by your death.

When everyone is in bed, do not, I repeat, DO NOT wander

around the house, randomly opening up bedroom doors in the middle of the night. Waking up to a short, bald man staring at you in the darkness is frightening for even the most stout of heart.

If by some miracle your midnight walkabouts have not resulted in you being tied to a tree, and you wake up in a warm bed the next morning, leave immediately. Do not, under any circumstances, stay for breakfast. Nobody wants to eat with you. They just want to forget they ever met you.

Let them.

Wardrobe Malfunction

There is a time and a place for wearing a sheer dress without a bra. It's called freshman year spring break in Cancun. Know what it's not called? Your daughter's wedding. I realize you spent good money on those D-cups, and I'm sure they are lovely, but do you really have to show them off *all the time?* Can't you take one day off? For your daughter's sake?

You might think that investing in nylon nipple covers makes going bra-less OK. You would be more wrong than you could ever know. Those things look like mini bullet-proof vests for your boobies, and they actually attract more attention than if you had just let everything hang loose.

And while we're on the subject of fashion, don't do multiple wardrobe changes throughout the wedding day. Everyone understands that you're excited about your daughter's union, but you're not hosting the Grammy's for god's sake. The dress you wore to the wedding is suitable for pictures, cutting the cake, *and* the reception. Plus, by changing every hour, you call attention to your clothing, making those hideous nipple patches that much more memorable. Besides, do you really want to be the reason that your daughter has to hide her R-rated wedding album?

Thin Walls

You just witnessed the wedding of your son. Love is in the air and liquor is in your bellies. Your emotions and hormones are on overdrive, but you're sharing the house with your son, his bride, and her parents. You might think you can have sex without anyone knowing, but you're wrong. Everyone will hear you and breakfast will be awkward. Don't do it.

Besides, once you reach a certain age you like to believe that your parents stopped having sex a long time ago. Everyone stands to benefit by maintaining this perception.

Everyone.

No You Didn't

I'm not sure how to begin this, so I'm just going to come right out and say it. Sex toys are inappropriate wedding gifts. I realize your sex therapist may have opened all sorts of doors for you and the bride's uncle, but the newlyweds are too young to be having problems in the bedroom.

Yes, you can have the present back.

Choose Your Adventure

You just had the best time at your friend's wedding, and you're setting up your tent to spend the night under the stars. You're pretty drunk, but feeling great. You met a hot girl from Vermont, and your chances of hooking up look strong. One of the grooms-men brought some psychedelic mushrooms and asks if you want some. This is the part where you choose your adventure, like in those books you used to read when you were a kid.

In adventure number one, you look at the hot girl from Vermont, who has the unmistakable "if he does mushrooms I'm not sleeping with him" look on her face. You politely thank the groomsman for offering you the mushrooms, but decline. He tells you "no problem," and walks away. You then take the hot girl back to your tent and the two of you bump uglies until the sun comes up. Then you do it again.

Her flight leaves that afternoon, so you volunteer to take her to the airport. You exchange contact information, and the follow-ing month you go out to Vermont to visit her. The magic contin-ues, and by the following summer you are engaged to the woman of your dreams. You get married, have beautiful children, and she wins twenty-million dollars in the lottery. You retire at age thirty-five, and sail your yacht around the world.

Yours is truly a charmed life.

In adventure number two, you try to convince the hot girl from Vermont to take the mushrooms with you. She calls you a druggie, and one of the other groomsmen takes her by the hand and leads her to his tent. Remember adventure number one? Well, that's his life now.

You follow the guy with the mushrooms into the forest, and the two of you split an ounce of the most potent fungus you've ever tried in your life. No more than a half-hour into your trip you are already being assaulted by interstellar goblins from planet Nebuloid who have eight arms, each of which has its own telepathic brain embedded in its palm. These creatures torment you for the better part of twelve hours with visions of the life you lost in adventure number one.

You wake up to the groom shaking you. You are immediately aware of the fact that you have pissed your pants. Apparently you were screaming for most of the night, preventing everyone else from getting any rest. The hot girl from Vermont has already left, and the few people who remain have little interest in speaking to you. For the next five years, you will draw cryptic sketches of aliens with eight arms. Your therapist will have no idea what they mean. You will lose your mind and jump off of the Golden Gate Bridge, only to be saved by the hot girl from Vermont's husband, who just happened to be sailing nearby in his new yacht. You have always been an atheist, but you are now convinced that there is a God, and he is punishing you.

Choose your adventure wisely.

Twisty Dick's Pickled Ear

The man looked like something a lawn mower had spit out. He was, in fact, sitting on a riding lawn mower, so I couldn't entirely rule out that possibility. His hands were deeply veined and encrusted with an unidentifiable filth. They trembled as he grasped the steering wheel of the John Deere mower, as if he were desperately clinging to the wheel of an accelerating sports car...or his sanity.

I first noticed the bizarre man as I approached the liquor store in Paonia, a small mountain town in Colorado. I was visiting my friend Mickey for a three-day weekend of fly fishing and binge drinking, so I had come to stock up on beers for the next few days. "Young man," he whispered to me from beneath a nearby conifer. "Psst...Young man, you seen my ear anyplace?" I looked to see if he was missing an ear, but I couldn't see past the grimy mop that was masquerading as his hair.

Not sure what to make of his remark, I shot him a puzzled glance and continued walking. "Do your good deed for the day and buy this old cripple some whiskey to kill the pain of his combat wounds," he went on. "I'll even give ya some extra money to buy yerself somethin' nice. Here, have a look-see." He reached into the front pocket of his ragged overalls and eagerly withdrew a fistful of wadded bills, no doubt contaminated by the same anonymous sludge that saturated his greasy beard and every mottled inch of his skin. He triumphantly held the money high above his head as if it were some ancient artifact he had unearthed after a life-long search. I wondered how many diseases I might contract should any portion of one of those bills come into contact with my skin.

He was definitely an eccentric, maybe even a nutjob, but his seemed like a reasonable request. The homeless drunks I encountered in the city were always asking for money. This guy just needed someone to go inside and facilitate the transaction, just as I had asked so many adults to do when I was a teenager in need of booze.

As I sometimes do when trying to justify giving money to panhandlers, I began to construct a fictional reality in my mind for this man. He claimed to be a war veteran—and a cripple to boot, which meant that he should be wheel-chair bound. *But the social security and disability checks were so small, if they even came at all, that the purchase of a motorized wheel-chair was out of the question. The poor bastard must have improvised this antiquated lawn mower to get him around.*

I glanced around the landscape to give my mind a break from this grim fantasy. This was the picturesque Western Slope of Colorado. It was a sunny afternoon in early October, and the damp chill in the breeze whispered of wintry blusters that would soon rip through the valley. Soon, the leaves from the deciduous trees lining the banks of the nearby Gunnison River would fall to the ground. Then, winter storms would blanket the landscape with snow—sometimes several feet at a time. I imagined the man's overturned mower stuck in a snowdrift in late November, his filthy body half-submerged in the freezing snow. He might lay there for hours before anyone found him, if they found him at all. The dull ache of old war wounds would be his only companion as he longed for a bottle of spirits to numb the pain.

The door of the liquor store slammed shut—jerking me out of my wintry fantasy and placing me firmly back in the present moment. I noticed that there were only two neon signs in the window: *Grolsch* and *Jagermeister*. I searched for a wheelchair ramp, trying to suppress the judgment that was rapidly growing in my mind. But the only way inside I could see was up the three concrete steps leading to the front door. *Nazi bastards,* I thought. *Probably still bitter about getting their asses kicked in the war. You're goddamn right I'll buy this war hero some booze.*

But as I made my first resolute step toward the old man, my friend Mickey, a life-long resident of this small town, grabbed me by the arm and jerked me back towards the store. "What do you think you're doing?" he demanded. "Nobody buys liquor for Twisty Dick. The bastard probably ran out of yeast for his home-made moonshine, and is having one of his withdrawal fits. The liquor store stopped selling to him years ago..." Mickey stopped for a moment and looked down at his shoes, "...after the llama incident. Anyway, he's been camping out here ever since. Every once in a while he'll find some out-of-town sucker like you to buy him a bottle. The next thing you know, he'll be trying to summit Mount Lamborn on that goddamn mower, wearing nothing but his underwear and a stocking cap."

I meant to ask Mickey about his obvious role in the llama incident, but as we roamed the isles of booze I was soon caught up in his account of the old man's life. According to Mickey, Twisty Dick was a Golden Glove boxer in the Navy during World War II. After the war ended, he and his Navy buddies found themselves in a rowdy bar on the South side of Chicago. Twisty Dick had just discovered that while he was away at war, his wife had cheated on him with a draft-dodging professor from Loyola. Upon hearing the news, the broken-hearted veteran downed half a bottle of scotch and set out to find an excuse to showcase his trusty one-two. That night he found some marines with enough brass to take him on, and according to Mickey's version of the story, Twisty laid three of them out cold—but not before one of the cowards gnawed off a considerable chunk of his ear.

The police soon came, and Twisty and his friends had to high-tail it out of the bar. That evening, Twisty was on the next train to Colorado. In his haste to avoid the cops, Twisty forgot to go back to the bar and collect what was left of his ear. He never returned to Chicago. Thinking the appendage might be a novelty to the patrons, the bartender put the gnawed hunk of flesh in a jar of pickling juice. According to Mickey, there it remains to this day.

Mickey says that if one were in search of a truly unique experience, they could go to that bar in Chicago and the bartender will infuse a shot of their choosing with an ounce of Twisty Dick's pickled-ear juice—provided, of course, they recite the sacred toast...

Here's a toast to Twisty Dick, the only man with a corkscrew prick,

Spent his day on the hunt, looking for the girl with a corkscrew cunt.

When he found her, Dick dropped dead.

Dirty bitch had a left-hand thread.

May warts and corns adorn your feet,

May crabs the size of elephants climb upon your balls and feast.

When you're old and feeble and in a helluva wreck,

May your head fall through your asshole and break your goddamn neck.

Nobody knows if the story is true, or who created the words to the toast, but around Paonia, Colorado, it's recited around campfires with near religious fervor. In keeping with tradition, that night we drank to the old veteran. We saluted his corkscrew prick, and hailed his trusty John Deere steed. We lamented his severed ear, and cursed the dirty bitch who had left him so utterly alone. As I looked up at the stars, I couldn't focus my thoughts on anything but old Twisty Dick. I imagined him gazing at the same night sky, alone, replaying memories of wartime carnage, a lonely bottle of moonshine his only refuge from the fire and death that had never stopped falling from the beautiful, dark sky.

FROM THE DESK OF PIMP DADDY "J"

DATE: _____ SUBJECT: _____

Twisty Dick's Pickled Ear

Hey Broseph,

I just finished the drawing I told you about. You know the one one with the guy who has a twisty dick? Holding a jar with a chunk of his ear in it, soaking in pickle juice? I'm sure you remember. But really, I think this fits your story quite well. You have your retired war veteran, drunk, drunk as piss, tatted up from wrist to shoulder on his right arm, long dirty hair, long dirty beard, wearing army pants, ghetto gloves, and a wife beater. He's standing infront of the liquor store, with his riding lawn mower parked in a handy capped spot, waiting for a sucker like you to buy him some whiskey. When did you become so gullible, anyway? Good thing you had Mickey there to set your ass straight.

Sincerely,
Jared

Reclaiming Cider Creek

Part I – Cider Creek

A family of tall, strong cottonwood trees lined the creek that ran behind our house in Omaha. Between the unremarkable, lime-colored cottage we rented and that stream was a vast field of uninterrupted prairie grass that stretched on for longer than I could hit a baseball. After school most days, I would take my dog, Emma, down to Cider Creek and sit under the shade of the enormous trees while she happily splashed in the cold water. I was a lonely, fifteen year-old kid, and she was my best friend.

The banks of Cider Creek were steep from centuries of springtime floods, and the canopy of the trees overhead was thick, so when I reached the bottom of the bank and closed my eyes, the only sound I could hear was the flash of the stream over smooth stones and the chorus of the many birds that inhabited the trees. It was the most peaceful place I knew. I went there frequently— sometimes to relish some sweet personal victory, but mostly to get away from my parents' arguing. The spot was all-mine. In the four years I lived in that house I never saw anyone else there, except for Emma, of course.

The city council had recently approved a plan to install a bike path alongside the creek, which I initially thought was a terrible idea. I feared that before long, hoards of people would descend on the landscape with their noisy lives and interrupt the stillness of my hideout. Soon, however, I realized that I was being selfish, and acknowledged that places as special as Cider Creek should be shared with everyone. Besides, I figured my days passing time by the creek were probably numbered.

I was going to turn sixteen at the end of the week, and my dad had already bought me my first car—an eleven-hundred dollar Ford Taurus that ran on only three of its four cylinders. The decal on the rear fender said "Limited Edition," so I named her "L.E." Once I got my driver's license, the odds that I would be spending much time down by the creek were slim. I only had three days to go before my birthday, and I waited anxiously for the time to pass. That day, the city dropped off a series of large pieces of machinery in the field behind our house. It seemed like a lot of muscle for putting in a simple bike path, but I didn't give it much thought—I was too excited about being able to drive.

When my birthday finally arrived, I was so excited I could barely contain myself. If all went according to plan, I would be driving that afternoon, which could only bode well for my dismal social life. I had grown six inches the prior summer, and I was now tall and lean, so the girls were slowly starting to pay attention.

Once I got my license I could get a girlfriend—maybe even take her for rides into the country. Emma could come too. We'd find a new stream for Emma to play in, and I'd do some fishing. My new girlfriend would make a picnic and we'd all sit down by the river bank, relaxing in the warm sunshine. At least, that's how I pictured it.

On the day of my birthday, my dad picked me up early from school. He made some excuse about forgetting my birth certificate at home, so we stopped there before going to my driver's exam. Before we left for the DMV, he sat me down in the living room. He said we needed to talk.

At first I thought he was going to have the typical "driving is a privilege" conversation with me—the kind you see on all of those bubblegum sitcoms on TV. But my dad was never one for those kinds of talks. This felt different. He looked uncomfortable, the way a doctor looks before he delivers very bad news to a wife or a son—the kind of news that turns lives upside-down.

"Son, before we leave, there is something I need to tell you," he began. "You're probably going to want to sit down."

"Dad, I already told you that I'm going to be careful with the car. I really appreciate you buying it for me, and I'm not going to wreck it or anything. I swear."

He let out one of those nervous, sputtering laughs, and in his eyes I could see something was troubling him. He was holding a manila folder, and as he fumbled with it, I could see that his usually steady hands were slightly shaking. He had calloused hands from a life of hard labor, and that sterile-looking folder seemed oddly out of place in his grasp. We hadn't talked much over the years, but we had spent a lot of time together, and we always knew when something was wrong with the other. We didn't do a lot of fun activities together like camping and that sort of thing, but we had a special, unspoken bond. My dad was probably my best friend—he and Emma.

"I know, son. You're a good kid." He cleared his throat. "Could you please sit down for me? It's important that I tell you this now." I swallowed hard and remained standing. I wasn't a disobedient kid, but I guess somehow I subconsciously thought that if I stayed standing up, I could prevent the delivery of whatever bad news was coming.

"Are you OK, Dad?" I asked. "Is it the thyroid thing again? You're not dying, are you? The doctor said you were going to make a full recovery."

My eyes began to swell with tears. My parents had just gotten back together after a messy, three-year separation during which time I had lived in a cramped, one bedroom apartment with my mom and my sister. I had just gotten my dad back and I couldn't imagine losing him again.

"No, Ryan. I'm not dying," he replied. "Could you please just sit down? I don't know how to do this." He sounded desperate. I reluctantly sat on the old, blue recliner, hoping that doing so would erase the terrible look on his face. It didn't. "I want you to know that what I'm going to say doesn't change anything." He took a deep breath before he went on.

We had started a lawn service out of the trunk of our '78

Oldsmobile two years before. One warm, spring afternoon, I accidentally ran over a baby bunny with one of our commercial mowers. It wasn't an uncommon thing to have happen—adult rabbits make shallow dens in the grass, and it's hard to know where they are until it is too late. The blades had flung the rabbit into the middle of the road where it painfully twitched and spasmed. I remember a woman was walking her daughter through the park across the street when it happened. The two of them watched in horror as my dad approached the quivering bunny with a stick, took a deep, strained breath, and bashed the rabbit's head in, ending its misery.

The deep breath my dad took before killing that bunny was exactly the same as the one he took before he spoke again.

"When your mom was very young, she met a man...and they, well, she got pregnant." He paused, telling me the rest with his eyes. It was as if he were begging me to understand so that he didn't have to speak the rest. Still, he went on.

"That child was you. The man...well, he wasn't me. He was also very young, and he left your mom shortly after you were born. I met her when you were still a baby, and I raised you ever since. I loved you like you were mine—you *are* mine."

I felt like someone had driven a truck through my chest. I cried one of those silent sobs that hollows you out and makes you feel as if some beast is greedily devouring your insides. When the air returned to my lungs, it brought anger. Emma entered the doorway, cautiously wagging her tail and cowering. "Get out of here!" I yelled at her. She tucked her tail and retreated downstairs with a whimper.

"You...you lied to me my whole life," I accused my dad. Outside I heard the sound of diesel engines and the beeping sound of large trucks backing up. I had never yelled at my dad like this before, and for a moment my vulnerability subsided, and I felt as powerful as the machinery in the field outside.

"Ryan, I told you this doesn't change anything. We were just trying to protect you—the last thing we wanted to do was to hurt you. Please, son, I love you." He held out his arms to embrace me.

"Well, you did hurt me, Dad," I said as I backed away from his reach. "Why wait all of this time? You do this on my sixteenth birthday—what kind of sick shit is that?"

He looked down at the file folder in his hands, pulled out a sheet of paper, and handed it to me without a word. He stared silently at the floor as I read the birth certificate.

"You mean to tell me I have a different last name than all of you?" My mind was racing, trying to process everything at once. Then, suddenly, it became clear. "You weren't going to tell me, were you? You *had* to tell me because I couldn't get my driver's license without my birth certificate."

He looked up at me with affirming eyes, tears flowing down each side of his rough face. Outside I heard a loud crunching sound, like a car crash, only in slow motion. I didn't know what it was, but it sounded as angry and destructive as I felt. I crumpled up the birth certificate, threw it at the wall, and raced out the front door, toward the sound.

There was only one place in the world I wanted to be at that moment, the only place that could help me feel whole again—my spot down by Cider Creek. I ran there as hard as I could, blinded to the backhoes and bulldozers and men in hard hats I passed along the way. I was so consumed with emotion that I didn't notice this new tragedy until it surrounded me.

Bulldozers were tearing down the majestic cottonwoods that enclosed my refuge. Birds fearfully scattered across the sky as their homes, one by one, fell to the ground with grotesque sounds of finality. Fluffy cottonwood seeds floated everywhere. The wonderful scent of freshly-hewn wood mixed unpleasantly with the noxious fumes of diesel engines.

On any other day I might have thrown my body in front of the bulldozers to save this beautiful place, but I wasn't thinking clearly. I felt a severe vertigo overtake my body, and I thought for a moment that I might pass out or vomit. I fought the feeling, swallowed my anguish, and started to sprint through the construction zone, heading upstream. One of the workers yelled at me and tried to grab my arm, but I dodged him and ran even faster toward the creek. I reached the bank in a single leap, landing on my familiar foot path.

I ran so hard for so long that my lungs burned as if all of the oxygen along the creek had been replaced by the thick, black smoke of the diesel trucks I had just escaped. As I ran, my dad's words kept repeating in my mind. *I loved you like you were mine...*

One emotion consumed me above all others: terror. I felt as if the events of that day had been conjured by some unknown evil from my worst nightmares, and if I kept running, I might somehow escape the truth.

The truth was, that despite what my dad wanted me to think,

he wasn't my *dad*. This was the last thought that passed through my mind before I collapsed on the bank of the stream.

I woke up some hours later, in the twilight, my body half submerged in the water, and shivering. Emma was licking my face and nervously whining. She must have waited until my dad let her outside, jumped the fence, and followed my scent. "Good girl," I told her. I was so glad to see my friend. The sun was setting quickly, and I had no idea where I was. I climbed the bank to have a look around.

About a hundred yards upstream was a small bridge. Emma and I crossed it, and walked east along the county road until I saw an old farmhouse with its lights on. I didn't have a plan. All I knew was that I wasn't going to sleep down in that creek. This was already the worst birthday I had ever had, and the thought of sleeping on the cold, muddy banks was unbearable. I knocked on the door of the farmer's house and asked if he would call my parents. I heard him tell my dad that I was fourteen miles southwest of our house. The distance felt much further.

Part II – Operation Pervmeister

Twelve years later, my voice trembling, I told this same story to my thirteen-year-old brother and watched his eyes fill with tears. Forgotten visions of lifeless bunnies, my dad's shaky hands, and uprooted cottonwoods came rushing back to me. I tried to explain to him, as our dad had to me, that this information didn't change anything—that we were still brothers. But he knew that it did change things. It didn't change how we felt about each other, as I had eventually learned myself years before, but it would change the way he looked at his humanity. That day, he learned that there are secrets in this life that have the power to uproot you, to take everything that is safe and familiar to you and rip it out of the ground.

After our talk, I took him to a College World Series baseball game where we ate funnel cakes and corn dogs. It was sort of a cruel strategy—to tell him life-altering news and then take him to a place where everyone was having a good time. But the atmosphere allowed both of us to relax a bit, so I suppose it worked. I told myself that it was better than going home where he would most likely go to his room to sulk by himself. I didn't want him to be alone.

"So, how come you decided to tell me today?" He asked after nearly four innings of silence. "The only reason dad told you was because of your driver's license, so there must be a reason that you told me, right?"

God, this kid's sharp, I thought. "Well, Jesse," I answered, "you know that I'm getting married next month, right? Well, *he's* going to be there." I looked him in the eyes, and he got the point.

"You mean your dad?"

"No," I corrected. "Dad's my dad. What I mean is that my biological father is going to be at the wedding. And you're a groomsman, so you're going to meet him."

"But, didn't he, like, abandon you when you were a baby? I wouldn't think that you would ever want to talk to him again.

Why have him at your wedding?"

I went on to explain how complicated adult relationships can be. How, sometimes, people unintentionally hurt each other and regret it for the rest of their lives. I told him that sometimes people deserve a second chance. I tried not to patronize him by telling him that he would understand when he grew up, but that was the truth. I hated myself for sounding the same way grownups sounded when I was a kid.

On the drive home things seemed to be OK. We were laughing and joking, and though beneath that levity there was an element of sadness, it seemed distant and mostly benign. There was no question we had both experienced better College World Series games, but given the circumstances, I felt the day had turned out as best as could be expected.

When we arrived at my parents' house, my brother gave me a casual fist bump of gratitude, and went downstairs to his room. I went into the kitchen and debriefed my parents. They had initially been apprehensive about letting me tell my brother, but I assured them that if history was any indicator about their ability to break bad news, everyone would be better off by letting me take a crack at it. In my book, corn dogs and a baseball game beat a missing person's report any day.

I went home the next day to finish planning my wedding, assured that I had handled the situation as best as I could have. But soon after I left, my parents told me that they had caught Jesse sneaking out of the house late at night. The night he came home with a hickey on his neck my mom called me in tears. "I'm the worst mother on the planet!"

"Well, that's just ridiculous," I replied. "Have you met every mother on the planet? I read the other day that mothers in New Delhi sell their daughters into prostitution as soon as they start menstruating. I'm sure you're a better mom than some of them." I could feel her trademark sneer through the phone.

My brother snuck out of the house several more times in the following two weeks, and despite my parents' warnings and his eventual grounding, nothing could deter his behavior. Soon my parents became genuinely concerned for his safety. After all, he was a thirteen-year-old kid wandering the streets with his friends in the middle of the night. While Omaha was no Harlem, it had all the crime and problems of a big city, and it certainly wasn't a safe place for kids to explore in the middle of the night.

"What if he gets picked up by one of those perverts?" My mom asked me on the phone one night. "I saw a special on Oprah about these sickos who drive around in vans and pick up kids like your brother who sneak out of the house. They do gross things to them. *Perverts.*"

My mom, like so many American women, is infatuated with Oprah. It doesn't matter what Oprah says, ask any housewife and she will tell you that Oprah is infallible. Personally, I'm suspicious of anyone who can run a marathon and go up six dress sizes in the same year. Anyway, her segment on perverts gave me an idea about how we could put an end to my brother's clandestine activities.

It was a week before my wedding ceremony, and anyone who

192

has ever planned their own wedding can tell you that the last week before the event is easily the most chaotic. If something can go wrong, it almost certainly will. Flowers, food, liquor, DJ, lodging—you name it. You know you're marrying the right woman when you tell her she has to manage it all single-handedly while you leave to sort out your dysfunctional family issues, and she doesn't go Bridezilla on your ass.

I arrived at my parents' house on a Friday morning. "How is your progress with *Operation Pervmeister?*" I shouted to my mom from the front door as I removed my shoes. "We don't have much time."

"Huh?" She yelled back from the kitchen with her ditzy housewife inflection. "Did someone say perverts? Did you finally see the Oprah episode? Those *perverts* are so *gross.*"

"He means, did you find out when his brother plans on sneaking out again," my dad clarified from the living-room couch as he rolled his eyes in my direction.

"Oh, shut up, Virgil. What do you know?" She snarled as she hacked up a phlegm ball from the back of her throat and swallowed it back down again. "I didn't like going behind his back and snooping through his text messages, but yes, I found out. His friend is spending the night here tonight. They are planning on sneaking out to meet some girls down at the park. I felt so terrible about invading his privacy like that."

"Yes, mom, you're absolutely right. Heaven forbid you invade your teenage son's privacy in order to protect him from all of those crazed, child-molesting perverts roaming the streets late at night. If only Oprah could hear you now." I turned to my dad, "Were you able to borrow your buddy's van?"

"Sure was. I've got it parked down at my shop. You're not planning on doing what I think you are—are you?"

"Yes, Ryan—what *are* you planning?" My mom demanded.

"If I'm not mistaken," my dad answered, "I think our oldest son wants us to help him kidnap our youngest son."

"Bingo," I said with a smile.

"What?" My mom screeched. "Nobody is going to be kidnapping anybody—this is insane! I need to go turn on one of my Dr. Wayne Dyer tapes. He's so wise. He'll have some guidance for us."

My mom can be one of the most obtuse people you'll ever encounter. Arguing with her can be like having a staring contest with a brick wall. Sure, you can try it, but at the end of the day, one of you is going to be a brick wall and the other is going to be a loser.

Over several decades of vigilant study, I have discovered that in order to get your way with my mom, all you have to do is make a compelling argument that either Jesus, Oprah, or one of her evangelical ministers whose audio tapes she religiously listens to would agree with your point of view. Oh, and sometimes, oddly enough, Howie Long, the former NFL football player, is a viable alternative. My mom thinks he's a real man, and she has no qualms about telling my dad how profoundly, and in how many ways, he will always fall short of the perfection that is Howie Long.

It took a dash of Howie, Oprah and Jesus rhetoric, but I eventually convinced my mom to be an accomplice in the kidnapping of her own son. With everyone on-board with my plan, it was time to make some last-minute purchases at the store. We didn't have much time, and there was much to buy. By my calculations, the following items were the bare minimum we needed to kidnap my brother and his friend: three black ski masks, a package of pork chops, some rope, a couple of blindfolds, a mini propane torch, some scrap wood, a pair of long-distance walkie-talkies, and a package of popsicles, preferably JELLO Pudding Pops. I was going to have to rely on two decades worth of kidnapping and torture scenes from my favorite action/adventure movies to pull this off.

I had just made it home from the store with all of the supplies, when the smell of burnt chicken and the sight of boxed potatoes au gratin told me that my mom had finished making dinner. My brother had invited his friend over to eat with us, so I set out to see what sensitive information I could extract from them. "So, guys, any big plans for the evening?" I half-heartedly asked, not wanting to show too much interest. They looked at one another, exchanged smirks of self-satisfaction, and shrugged their shoulders.

"Nah, not really," they said, almost in unison.

"Really?" I responded incredulously. "Two young, strapping boys on the very cusp of manhood, their whole lives in front of them, and no plans on a Friday night? I would have thought you guys would have girls lining up at the back door to get their hands on you." At that moment my brother's cell phone chimed to indicate a new text message. He read it and handed the phone to his friend to see. They both giggled. They seemed certain that we were completely in the dark about their plans. In a few hours, once *Operation Pervmeister* hit them, they would find out just how wrong they were.

It was going to be a long night, so I decided to take a nap after dinner. Our intel told us that the boys were going to meet a group of girls at the park at 0130 hours. The park was two miles away, so they needed to leave by 0100 hours to arrive on-time. I instructed my parents to be up and dressed by 0030 hours just in case the kids tried to leave early. This was, of course, confusing for my mother, so I had to eventually stop using military time.

As I predicted, we heard the boys sneak out through my brother's window and jump the fence at 12:45 a.m. I had to move quickly if I was going to beat them to their destination. I hopped on my brother's bike, walkie-talkie in hand, while my parents took the van, which my dad had parked two blocks away.

"Ghostrider One, this is Glorious Falcon, do you copy?" I painfully yelled into the walkie-talkie as my knees hit the handle bars of the adolescent bike with every revolution of the pedals.

"Uh, Ryan, is that you?" I heard a voice stumble back to me over the radio. "Virgil, I think it's Ryan. Who's Ghostrider? Hello?"

"Goddammit, Mom, you're screwing this up." I scolded. "Put Dad on."

"Glorious Falcon, roger that," he responded with a laugh. It sounded like my dad was actually enjoying this operation, which made me wonder: after all the stress children cause their parents, how often do parents entertain twisted fantasies about inflicting permanent psychological and/or physical damage upon their kids? My suspicion was that the answer to that question was more often than I'd like to know. I told myself this was noble work—I was helping realize my parents' dreams.

"Copy that." I responded. "Remember, I will arrive at the rendezvous point, secure a tactical vantage position, and pounce at the appropriate time. Commence radio silence in 3, 2, 1. Glorious Falcon, out."

When I arrived at the park, the girls Jesse was supposed to meet were already there. I could hear them smacking their gum and loudly complaining because the boys were making them wait. I hid my brother's bike in a nearby but secluded bush. I then climbed a tall cottonwood that allowed me to see and hear what was happening below.

"Like, oh my god, Christy," one girl said to the other. "This is so lame. We're princesses. They're lucky we're even here, and they have the audass...the audassity—like, the *nerve* to make us wait?"

After making me endure no less than five minutes of this inane, mind-warping blather, my brother and his friend finally showed up. I resisted the temptation to immediately descend upon them—I wanted to find out what they were up to first. Right away, I saw my brother pull out a bottle of some kind of alcohol and pass it to one of the girls, who took a drink. The girl passed the bottle to her friend, and kissed my brother. The scene took me back to my younger days when I pined for the affections of girls like Amber Anderson, and for a moment, I thought about abandoning the plan.

I had done the exact same thing when I was young—wasn't I being a hypocrite for breaking this up? Then I remembered that he was just an eighty-five-pound kid. What he was doing was dangerous, and as his big brother, it was my duty to set him straight. Besides, this was going to be fun. I took a deep breath, turned the volume on the walkie-talkie to its lowest level, and whispered, "Ghostrider One, do you copy?"

"Virgil, the thing is talking again." I heard my mother say. "No, you talk to him. Oh shut, up, you *fool*. You're not a real man. Howie Long, now that's a real man." After some shuffling and a handful of expletives, I heard my dad's voice. "Roger that, Glorious Falcon. We are in position."

"Copy. Maintain position. I'm going in."

I pulled the ski mask over my face, carefully climbed down the cottonwood, and crawled through the grass until I was twenty yards from the kids. I took a deep breath and jumped up, screaming, "I'm gonna butt-fuck you little bastards into oblivion!"

The four of them screamed so loudly and at such a high pitch that, were you to play a tape recording of the screams to a blind man, he would tell you without equivocation that he was listening to four little girls. The two actual girls immediately ran for cover, but for some reason, my brother and his friend didn't budge. I sprinted at the two boys, who remained frozen in their tracks, and tackled them hard onto the grass. For a moment I felt bad about hitting them so hard, but I told myself that they needed to think this was real. They both lay on the ground, motionless and gasping for air. I radioed to my dad, "Ghostrider One, I've got the package. Now! NOW!!"

Seconds later, the lights of the van at the bottom of the park turned on, the tires screeched, and the van rumbled up the hill to where I had the boys pinned to the ground. My mom slid open the side door, and I tossed each terrified boy inside, one after the other. By this time, the girls were probably halfway home. *Boy, do they have a story to share with their parents when they get home,* I thought.

Once inside the van, I quickly blindfolded the boys and bound their hands and feet with rope. Once they were secure, I knocked twice on the inside wall of the van to signal to my dad to start driving home. My brother's friend was bawling hysterically and calling for his mother. "Your mother's not going to save you from me, little boy," I screamed at him in the deepest, scariest voice I could muster. *Listen to yourself, Ryan. You truly have psychological problems,* I thought.

"Oh yeah?" Jesse shot back. "Well, my brother's going to come and kill you, you—psychopath! He's like crazy, superhero strong and he's gonna mess you up! Now untie me!" he demanded.

I couldn't help but smile. "This brother of yours sounds like an interesting guy," I replied. "Let's talk more about him. So he's a huge badass, huh?" My mom smacked me in the shoulder and frowned.

"Ahem, never mind that," I continued. "Badass or not, your brother has no idea where you are because you boys snuck out tonight, didn't you? That's right. You're all alone. On a random note, you boys don't happen to watch Oprah, do you?"

"What? Oprah? Screw that!" Jesse yelled. "My mom watches that faggoty shit. Do we look like queers to you, you sicko?"

It took all the strength I possessed to keep from laughing. *Who is brave enough to talk like that to his child-molesting captor while blindfolded and bound in the back of a creepy van?* I thought. "You've got a dirty little mouth on you boy, and I'm gonna fix that for ya'. I'm that guy they talk about on Oprah—the one that goes around kidnapping and torturing little boys all over the country." I excitedly winked at my mom, who frowned.

Meanwhile, Jesse's friend lay in the corner of the van, incoherently whimpering and attempting to recite what sounded like Psalm 23. "Yea, I...I'm l-like walking through Death Valley's shadow...and he's evil. The Oprah pervert is evil..."

I fired up the propane torch and laughed maniacally. "The torch has always been my favorite tool, boys. You see, it burns so hot—twenty-five hundred degrees—that it kills all of your nerve endings. You won't feel any pain—at first. You'll just feel ice cold. You can actually smell the flesh melting before you feel the pain. Who wants to try it first?"

I rolled my brother's friend on his stomach, and signaled for my mom to take out a popsicle and press it against his back. I held the torch over one of the pork chops, searing the meat. By this time, my dad had driven the van back to our house and pulled it into the garage. This was probably a bad idea because Jesse's friend thought I was cooking him to a well-done crisp, and was screaming at the absolute top of his lungs.

"Gag him or get him outta' here—do something!" My dad ordered, fearful that the neighbors would wake up and call the police.

"Fine," I responded. "But don't think I'm finished with you kid. Not by a long shot." I untied the boy's ropes, lifted him out of the van, and led him inside where I undid his blindfold and took off my ski mask. Before he could say anything I whispered, "Shh, shh, shh. It's okay, little buddy. We just pulled a little prank on you. You're safe." I handed him the popsicle. "Nothing's wrong with your back. Now, here is how this is going to go down. You're not going to tell your parents what happened here tonight and in exchange, I won't be telling them how we caught you doing drugs and having sex with those girls in the park."

"B-B-But, we weren't h-h-having…my parents won't b-believe…"

"No buts," I interrupted. "I just used a popsicle and a pork chop to convince you that I was the Oprah pervert who was burning a hole in your back with a torch. You actually think you're going to outsmart me? Look at yourself. Did you actually pee your pants? Honestly, kid. Go clean yourself up and count your blessings that what happened tonight wasn't for real. I've got to go have a talk with my brother."

Some people have guilty pleasures like overindulging on chocolate or watching too much Oprah. I learned that night that mine is blackmailing terrified children who I have just pretended to kidnap.

I put my mask back on and returned to the van. When I opened the door and looked at my frail brother tied up on the floor, blindfolded and trembling, it occurred to me that maybe, just maybe, I had taken this prank a little too far. I needed to wrap this thing up quickly, but not without getting my point across.

"Listen, kid," I accidentally began in my real voice. I could see tears streaming down his face. I re-adjusted my voice to sound like a scary pervert. "I scared you pretty good tonight, huh?" He didn't answer. "You, uh, mentioned your brother earlier. If you don't make it out of here alive tonight is there anything you'd want to say to him and the rest of your family?" He sniffed and waited before replying.

"I'd tell them that even though they do things that hurt me sometimes, I really love them a lot. And I'm sorry I've been sneaking out lately. If anything happens to me it will kill them, and it will all be my fault. Please let me go." I pulled off my mask and smiled at my parents. *Operation Pervmeister* was a success.

"That's a very mature point of view, young man. You know, I think I've had my fair share of perversion for a lifetime. Yep. I'm not sure I'm up for it any more. Maybe I'll get into animal torture or something, but child perversion—eh—to tell ya the truth, it's just losing its *oomph,* you know what I mean? I've got a proposition for you. If I were to let you and your friend go, would you promise not to be mad at your parents and your brother anymore?" I made a prayer gesture to my parents.

"Are, are you serious?" He said in disbelief. "Yeah, I'd forgive them for sure."

"Wonderful. That's fantastic news. O...K. Whaddya say we wrap this up, kiddo? I'm going to untie you now, so just relax and sit still." After I removed the rope from his limbs, I told him he could remove his blindfold. "But, do it slowly. This might be a bit of a shock." He took off the blindfold and when he opened his eyes he froze for at least five seconds, absolutely dumbfounded. "Care for a popsicle?" I said with a smile, offering him the box. "Or perhaps a pork chop—this one's almost done."

"You dick!" He screamed, his face bright red. "I'm going to kill you!" Apparently it was obvious that I was the mastermind behind this plot, because he completely ignored my parents, threw the blindfold at my face, and chased me around the yard, spitting cuss words like an automatic weapon.

"What about forgiveness?" I implored. "You promised that if I let you go you would forgive me and mom and dad. You promised!"

"Yeah, that was when I thought you were a perverted kidnapper who was going to kill me!" He continued chasing me around the yard.

"Completely irrelevant!" I barked back. "A promise is a promise!" The lights turned on in the house across the street.

"Hey, keep it down, dammit! It's the middle of the night, for god's sakes!"

"Oh, blow it out your ass, Carl!" My dad yelled back. "We're having a family meeting here."

Yep, we sure are, I thought. I stopped to let my brother tackle me and pound me with some body shots. Then I rolled him over and tickled him until he begged for mercy. Then I tickled him some more. "You alright, buddy? I scared the holy bejeebers out of you, huh?"

"Yeah, I'm alright. That was the meanest prank ever, but now that it's over, it's pretty funny. I love you, bro."

"I love you too, man. You really thought I was going to come and save you? What, do you think I've got some sort of superhuman, psychic powers or something?"

"Shut up, dude. I was bluffing. Maybe I was hoping..."

"Well, I ended up coming to the rescue after all, didn't I? Who else do you know that would fake-kidnap you? That's brotherly love right there."

"You're so messed up, man."

"Yeah, you're probably right. It must be in the genes." I winked at him and smiled.

The Fried Twinkie Manifesto

If I were to tell you that Bugs Bunny once held a Tommy gun to my head and demanded I tell him my darkest secret, would you call me crazy? What if I were to say that my one-word response to that loveable wabbit was "Twinkies"—would you then slowly back away toward the nearest exit? Never mind where the cartoon icon got the gun (they've got black markets for that sort of thing), or his motivations for interrogating me (hey, a rabbit's got his reasons). Indulge me for a moment, and let's focus on the Twinkies. I lost a part of myself along the way, and I'm convinced that those delicious golden cakes have something to do with it.

Though I wouldn't go so far as to blame Twinkies for the many personal failures of my white-trash existence, those cream-filled bastards have been suspiciously present for far too many compromising moments of my life for me to call it coincidence. To make matters worse, it now appears that Twinkies have formed an unholy alliance with Facebook. The sole purpose of this partnership, it seems, is to broadcast to the masses the most embarrassing moments of my life by means of a seemingly never-ending series of Twinkie-related updates that somehow have saturated the collective memory of my friends and family.

I despise Facebook, so this sinister union was troubling to me on principle alone. I just don't see the appeal of the website. If I want to talk to my friends, I just pick up the phone and call them. I don't need to log-on to some social network and post a comment for the whole world to see. Don't get me wrong—I'm addicted to Facebook, which may be a contributing factor to my hatred of the site. But my addiction, like most addictions I suppose, stems from an unhealthy place. In my case, the primary culprit is jealousy. By some mysterious malfunction of the cosmic scales of justice, it seems that some of the most despicable and irresponsible people I have ever encountered are now wildly successful and seemingly happy. And Facebook is always there to rub it in my face.

My contempt began to mount the day I read the following status update:

Danny Cox: Just opened up my third franchise—yee haw! Daddy just moved up a tax bracket!!!

I'm not usually one to bemoan the successes of others, but this guy, Danny Cox, once microwaved a cat, for god's sake. And I'm not talking about a stray cat, either. This was somebody's pet. It was the end-of-year party at Bill Carson's house, and Danny had chased down a handful of psychedelic mushrooms with some bourbon. According to the buzz around school, after discovering that Bill's little sister's cat had pissed in his shoes, Danny tracked the kitty down and nuked it in the microwave as nonchalantly as if it were a bag of Orville Redenbacher. Had they ever recovered the cat's body, Danny might have taken his rightful place as the leader of a juvenile detention center gang. But the cat was never found, and somehow he was able to make the natural transition from capital punishment to entrepreneurship.

Danny's success story wasn't an isolated incident, either. Soon after joining Facebook I was inundated with friend requests from people whose untimely deaths I would have expected to have read about in the newspaper. But somehow, many of them were now enjoying lives I had always expected for myself. Former drug addicts were buying timeshares in the Bahamas. A jock who couldn't recite the Pythagorean Theorem in ninth-grade geometry class was now a particle physicist who had supposedly collaborated with Stephen Hawking. How was this possible? I was the one who had sacrificed most of his twenties to get the degrees that were supposed to have formed the foundation of a successful career. Yet, it was me who was clinging to a lowly contractor job most of my Facebook friends would have scoffed at.

Sensing an opportunity to strike me while I was vulnerable, the Twinkies reared their ugly, cream-filled heads. This time, they used a Facebook wall post from an old friend as their weapon of choice:

Matthew Conner: Hey, man! Long time no see! I was just in Hawaii for a board meeting, and we saw some drunk in our hotel get kicked out for boring a hole in a honeydew melon and going to town on the thing in the middle of the business lounge. Anyway, it reminded me of you at that sleepover in junior-high when my mom caught you with that Twinkie. Hilarious!

Needless to say, other Facebook friends who saw the ill-fated update before I had the chance to delete it—my parents and wife included—had quite a few questions about just what, exactly, his mom had caught me doing with the Twinkie in question. The story is actually pretty simple. I was a fourteen-year-old kid who could get aroused by a voluptuous rock if the light struck it just right, and Matt's mom was smoking hot. In retrospect, she was actually pretty white trash and her tanorexic skin had the texture of rawhide, but she had a rockin' body, and most importantly, she was in to me. It may be hard to believe that a thirty-something single mom can be attracted to a young kid, but if her sexual over-tures were any indicator; she wanted a slice of the Rye Bread.

Her advances started subtly and gradually intensified over time. A simple, "Ryan, can you zip me up?" the prior summer had now escalated to a, "My, Ryan, haven't we grown up to be a big boy?" Her hand rigorously stroked the crotch of my corduroy pants as she stared intently into my eyes, lulling me into what can only be described as a boner trance. Lucky for me, the stroking was interrupted abruptly when her son Matt yelled to her from the other side of the house, "Mom, where did you put all those éclairs we bought at the store? Me and Ryan are gonna want to grub on those tonight."

Three hours and two massive Bavarian cream-filled éclairs later, Matt was snoring in a recliner chair on the other side of the basement living room as I tried to meditate away the unrelenting erection his mother had inspired. Looking for anything to focus on that was not stiff and protruding through my pants, I concentrated on the greasy package of éclairs on the floor. It was a six pack, and Matt and I had each eaten two, so there were now two left in the plastic container. Hoping the activity would divert some of the blood back into my brain, I carried the package upstairs to put it back in the refrigerator.

I could feel the boner starting to subside as I reached the upstairs landing, but then I saw her. Matt's mom was a drunk, and the sight of her blacked out on the couch in the upstairs living room was nothing new. However, I had never before seen her passed out like this: wearing nothing but her sheer bra and panties, her leathery skin bathed in pure moonlight from the slightly-drawn curtains. A bottle of Bartles & Jaymes rested between her toned thighs. My boner, which had just begun to subside, now rose again like a triumphant phoenix, soaring ever upward. In a panic, I rushed to a nearby bathroom, slammed the door, placed the éclairs on the toilet seat, and tried to calm myself. I splashed my face with cold water, but I might as well have been fighting a forest fire with a squirt gun. Desperate, I looked around the bathroom for relief, and in that moment I saw for the first time the limitless possibilities of cream-filled pastries.

Once I got the idea into my head, there was no getting it out. The moment was so cliché that Bill Clinton might as well have been playing saxophone from the shower. I frantically opened the pop-tab plastic package like a crack fiend in need of a fix, grasped an éclair in each hand, and proceeded to make sweet—but nasty—love to the pastry in my right. Just as I was beginning to lose myself in the erotic creaminess of the Bavarian filling, however, Matt's mom stirred from her wine-cooler slumber and opened up the door to the bathroom. Shocked to see me vigorously thrusting my adolescent manhood through the end of the helpless éclair, she let out a scream. Frightened myself, I instinctively raised the éclair in my left hand and chucked it at her as hard as I could. The pastry exploded on impact, covering her face and much of her silky lingerie in creamy filling. She then drunkenly slipped on the cream-laced tiles and fell backwards onto the carpeted hallway floor. Afraid she may have hurt herself, I clumsily duck-hopped over to her with my corduroys around my ankles to see if she was OK.

It was at this moment, with his mother suspiciously covered in creamy goo and his pants-less friend standing over her, donning a mangled French pastry from his still-fully-erect penis, that Matt came upstairs to investigate the source of the scream. All that was needed to ensure permanent psychological damage was for a ball gag and a set of anal beads to conveniently fall from the hallway closet.

As I remember it, Matt managed only one word: "…Mom?"

I could have chosen to be angry at Matt for resurrecting this memory from the mental dungeon to which I had rightfully banished it years ago. But, to be fair, he was probably more severely traumatized by the event than I was. And to his credit, after I explained to him what had happened that night, he instantly forgave me and we remain friends to this day.

But I never again spent the night at his house.

Ryan Moehring: Hey, Matt. It's hard to express the pleasure it gives me to know that a melon-fucking drunk reminds you of me. And we get to share that knowledge with all of our friends and family here on Facebook. Isn't that wonderful? Hi grandma! Oh, and for the record, they were éclairs, not Twinkies. Give a guy some credit! Anyway, I hope all is well. Give your mom my regards.

Not long after nostalgically cruising down the proverbial Bavarian Cream Boulevard, another of my adolescent acquaintances reminded me of a different pastry-related story. This time, actual Twinkies—fried ones in fact—played the lead role. The Facebook post came from George, a guy I have known since around the time I sprouted my first armpit hair.

George Epstein: My gentile brother from another mother! I finally made it back home, and I'm at the Nebraska State Fair as we speak! I'm gonna eat a fried Twinkie and fend off imaginary cartoon adversaries in your honor. LMAO!!!

This story takes place the summer after my senior year of high school. George and I had planned to spend the weekend camping along the banks of the North Platte River, but after a scorching day of sub-par fishing we decided to head back early and check out the state fair. We parked George's jeep, smoked a bowl, and then walked into the fair grounds. Those dissolving mint breath strips had just become popular, and George passed me one as we approached the ticket booth. "In case we run into any hoes," he explained.

After purchasing a handful of ride tickets, we walked to the concessions area to grab a bite to eat. George went straight for the Gyro stand, but I've got a compulsive sweet tooth, so I looked around for something to satisfy that urge. I didn't walk far before finding something I had never heard of before: fried Twinkies. It's difficult to express just how much I enjoy sweet foods, so suffice it to say that there was no way I could walk past the stand without trying this new-found treat. I surveyed the pathetic-looking kid in the paper hat with pity before ordering two fried Twinkies from him. A couple of minutes later he dispassionately slid them across the counter as if he were handing me a piece of his already-relinquished soul. "Please take me with you," he seemed to say with his eyes, much in the same way chimpanzees do at the zoo. As I walked away I wondered how many wrong turns you had to take before ending up like him.

George wanted to ride the Ferris wheel, so we slowly made our way to the other side of the fairgrounds where the bigger rides were located. I devoured my first Twinkie in two minutes flat, but resisted eating the second because getting high has always given me the munchies and I knew I would get hungry again soon. As we approached the ride, I started to get sick to my stomach. I told

George that I wasn't sure if I wanted to go, but he assured me that I'd be fine. Lucky for us there was no line to get on to the Ferris wheel, and the kid running the control box was a stoner about our age who let us ride by ourselves.

But as our Ferris-wheel car ascended, it quickly became clear that I was not fine. At the highest point of the ride I could see miles of farmland in every direction, but I could only focus on the Twinkie in my hand. For a moment, I could have sworn that it spoke to me. *I'm gonna get you,* I thought I heard it say. I looked over at George, who was smiling blissfully, and said, "Dude, I'm freakin' out. I think my Twinkie just...threatened me."

George grabbed my forearm, pulled me close, and said, "Listen, buddy. Remember that breath strip I gave you earlier? Well, I don't want you to freak out, 'cuz we're eighty feet in the air right now, but it was laced with LSD." He paused for a moment to let the idea sink in. "Things are going to get crazy for a while, so you might as well just go with the flow. Whatever you do, don't fight it."

I tried to respond to George, to chastise him for not giving me the chance to decide the terms of my first hallucinogenic experience on my own, but I couldn't muster a response. The Twinkie had taken hold of me.

You ate my brother, he hissed from his newly-formed mouth. I watched as long fangs formed on either side of his sinister grin. *Now you must pay!*

Suddenly, apparitions of all the benevolent characters from the cartoons of my childhood began to emanate from the mouth of the Twinkie. Bugs Bunny with his Tommy gun, Papa Smurf,

Captain Caveman, the Thunder Cats, and all the Super Friends—everybody was there. They all swirled menacingly around my head, shouting insults and threats, and in the case of Bugs Bunny, firing rounds from his automatic weapon. In a panic, I threw up the safety bar of the Ferris wheel and started to climb down. "What in the fuck are you doing?!" George screamed.

"Getting out of here!" I shouted back. "Mumm-Ra and the Care Bears teamed up to steal He-Man's Power Sword, and they're trying to decapitate me. But it's not their fault, George. The Twinkie's making them do it."

"O...K.," replied George. "I know what's going on here. The acid's just got a hold of you. Come on, buddy, just get back up here and I'll take care of that Twinkie for you." He reached for my hand, but as he did the car shifted, and I slipped out before he could reach me. I was now hanging from the bottom of the rickety Ferris wheel car where passengers normally rest their feet, suspended at least 30 feet in the air, and rising higher.

"Get your ass up here, man!" George pleaded. "You're gonna kill yourself."

"No!" I yelled back. "Not while that maniacal Twinkie is up there. He's telling everyone that I destroyed planet Thundera, but it was really Skeletor who did it. Oh no! Now the Shirt Tales are coming with Gargamel, and they look really angry, George. I'm getting out of here."

George tossed the Twinkie out of the car. "See, buddy? It's all gone now. The evil Twinkie has plummeted to his death. Now, please give me your hand before you do too."

"Well," I shouted from below, "as long as you're sure he's

gone—" I reached for his hand, but as I did the car jerked again. I held on to the bottom of the car by one arm, swaying dangerously high above the ground. Below, a teenage girl noticed me and let out a scream. Her cry attracted a crowd, which gathered around the Ferris wheel. The muscles in my hands and forearms burned, and I wasn't sure how much longer I could hold on. Luckily, the stoner in charge of the attraction then came sprinting back from an obvious weed-smoking break, and stopped the Ferris wheel so that our cart was positioned just a few feet above the ground. George and I jumped safely down.

George sensed that we might be in trouble, and instinctively went on the attack. He didn't seem to be the slightest bit affected by the drugs. "Your goddamn ride just about killed my friend! When was the last time you guys had a safety inspection on this thing, anyway?" He didn't allow the kid to reply before going on. Now he was addressing the crowd. "This Ferris wheel is unsafe, people. And *that* kid is high on marijuana cigarettes." He pointed to the teenage worker, who held his hands up in unconvincing protest. "That's right! I smelled it on him when we first came here, and despite my better judgment, we rode anyway. Keep your kids away from the Ferris wheel, folks."

He grabbed me by the arm and stormed off with phony indignation. "George," I began after we were out of the crowd's earshot, "are you sure the Twinkie is gone? I know this sounds weird, but I…I sense his presence."

"Oh, no!" George screamed, violently grasping the front of my shirt with both of his hands. "He's back, Ryan. Run for your life!"

"Oh my god! Hide me, George!"

"I'm just kidding buddy. I couldn't help myself."

Ryan Moehring: George! My Hassidic homeboy! If the malevolent Twinkie returns with his hoard of cartoon cronies, just use your Care Bear Stare! But seriously, don't forget to have a fried Twinkie for me, for old time's sake.

After publicly admitting to having had drug-induced visions of menacing Twinkies and to having gotten caught making love to one, you might think that it couldn't get much worse when it comes to me and Twinkies. But it does. Now is probably a good time to mention that not all of my Twinkies stories are funny. In fact, this one is pretty sad. The story begins with the following Facebook post I saw one night:

Ashley Eckersley: The doctor told me that the baby will react to a flashlight if you press it up to your stomach. Needless to say, after an hour Paul had to take the flashlight away from me. So much fun!!!

This may seem, at first blush, to be just an innocent post—a rather cute one at that. And if it came from any other person it would have been. As it were, the person posting it was my high-school sweetheart, and for many years I had been very much in love with her. But despite my feelings, after we broke up I swore to allow her to live her life, unimpeded by me and my inability to let go of the past. We had recently become Facebook "friends," which was the first substantial communication between us in several years. As a result, her pregnancy was news to me, and it hit me harder than I might have expected.

I suppose the reason for my reaction had something to do with the way things ended between us. To our parents' mutual disappointment, we decided to attend the only college that had accepted both of us: the University of Nebraska. I returned from my political-science study group one day at the end of our freshman year to find Ashley crying on my bed. The reason she was crying, she told me, was because she was pregnant.

She was pregnant and wanted to have an abortion.

Both of these things are heavy topics to deal with on their own, let alone in the same sentence, and I found myself wanting to process them separately. My family made the Beverly Hillbillies look like the Rockefellers, so I was used to a sordid existence where everyone popped out at least one baby by the time they were eighteen. Heck, as far as they were concerned, I was way ahead of the responsibility curve. And though I was the family's college boy who was supposed to be the one to break the cycle, I loved Ashley more than I could ever begin to explain, and killing something that she and I had created just didn't seem like an option to me. I'm still not sure why I didn't tell her—probably because I had never seen her look so helpless—but at eighteen-years-old I wanted to raise a baby with her.

Ashley didn't share my white-trash heritage, however, and the topic wasn't up for debate. A pregnancy would have been unacceptable to parents who were already unhappy about paying tuition so that their daughter could consort with a blue-collar scrub like me. Besides, Ashley was so distraught over the pregnancy that I knew if I pushed her to reconsider; I might lose both her and the baby. In my selfish desperation, I told myself that sacrificing the child to keep the love of my life was somehow a victory.

As I look back, my reaction to the pregnancy was surprisingly pro-life. And though I didn't look at the world through a political lens at the time, I was then and still am now, rather socially liberal. You would be hard-pressed to label me as conservative in any way, in fact. I have fucked the unholy cream out of an éclair, for god's sake. I have jumped out of moving Ferris-wheel cars while tripping on acid to avoid the attacks of imaginary cartoon characters. I'd venture to say that I've lived a pretty liberal life, even by European standards. As a result, my reaction to the pregnancy was surprising even to me.

I convinced myself that my opinion on the matter was irrelevant. After all, it was her body and her choice. Who was I to pressure her into teenage pregnancy? I told myself things like "she's got her whole life in front of her" and "she's got so much to look forward to." Before I could fully process what was happening to us, Ashley had already made her decision. Neither of us had the $300 for the procedure, and we couldn't borrow it from our parents for fear that they would somehow discover our secret. That left it up to me to get a job. Not surprisingly, there are few opportunities for gainful employment when you're an unskilled college kid trying to raise abortion money, and after a week of searching, the only position I could find was working as a supervisor at a fried-food stand at the Nebraska State Fair—yes, the very same concession stand that sold me the malevolent Twinkie just one summer before. It's terrifying how quickly one's wrong turns can add up.

There are few things that can convince you of your unpreparedness to raise a child more than having to supervise a bunch of angsty, pimply-faced teenagers at a fried-Twinkie stand. But I only needed to endure this humiliation for about 10 days to raise the money, so I did what I could to artificially inflate my spirits. This usually entailed shouting encouragement to my band of rejects.

"Mitch! When that eight-year-old girl wins a blue ribbon for her Simmental Heifer, are you going to let her parents take her to the cafeteria to eat (gasp!) a salad? Not on my watch, son! You get in her parents' faces and question their judgment—their very parental authority, if that's what it takes to ensure that little girl gets her fried Twinkie."

"Johnny! Nothing brings children more joy than cheerfully munching on a fried Twinkie while watching Edmund Baptiste, Cheese Artiste bring their favorite animated character to life, right before their eyes. Only you can make that magic happen. Do it for the children, Johnny. The children are our future."

But these kids were about as happy as I was to be there, and in time, they soon ignored me as much as Ashley did. Between work and school, I saw Ashley less and less, and when I did see her, things were strained. I tried to talk to her about our situation, but whenever I did she just teared up and walked away. The last thing I needed was another awkward environment, so I made one last-ditch effort to improve the morale at work. I remembered that several of the kids claimed to be Communists (though I doubt they understood what that meant), and since I had just finished reading *The Communist Manifesto* in political-science class, I decided that writing a Marx-inspired manifesto for our fried Twinkies would not only appeal to their sociopolitical sensibilities, but would also allow us a temporary interlude from the unbearable weight of our collective self-loathing.

If you bought a fried Twinkie from our stand that final week I worked at the fair, these were the steps taken before we placed the finished product in your hands: we dropped the Twinkie in a week-old vat of congealed oil, where it floated for sixty seconds alongside half-a-dozen or so unlucky flies. Next, we shoved a wooden corndog stick in one end, covered the piping-hot pastry with powdered sugar, adorned it with a handful of chocolate sprinkles, and finally, wrapped the finished product in a piece of semi-transparent food paper bearing the full text of *The Fried Twinkie Manifesto*.

THE FRIED TWINKIE MANIFESTO

A Specter is haunting America—the specter of the fried Twinkie. All the powers of this great nation have entered into a holy alliance to exorcise this specter: The Commissioner of the Nebraska State Fair, the President of the American League of Fried Treats, NASCAR, and tailgaters everywhere.

Where is there a fried Twinkie facing discrimination that has not been decried as unhealthy by its opponents in power? Where is the organic, tree-hugging opposition that has not hurled back the branding reproach of fried Twinkies, against the more advanced opposition parties, as well as against its reactionary adversaries?

Two things result from this fact:

1. Fried Twinkies are already acknowledged by Americans to be themselves a healthy and delectable snack food.

2. It is high time that fried Twinkie enthusiasts should openly, in the face of the whole world, publish their views, their aims, their tendencies, and meet this nursery tale of the specter of the fried Twinkie with a manifesto of the snack itself.

To this end, fried Twinkie enthusiasts of all nationalities have assembled at the Nebraska State Fair this summer to share the gospel of fried Twinkies with the world. Let this manifesto light their way.

Fried Twinkie lovers disdain to conceal their views and aims. They openly declare that their ends can only be attained by the forcible overthrow of all dietary definitions. Let the nutritional bureaucrats tremble at a fried Twinkie revolution. We have nothing to lose but the food pyramid. We have a world to win.

FRIED TWINKIE LOVERS OF ALL NATIONS, UNITE!

It's been over a decade, and I'm embarrassed to admit that I still dream about those days. These dreams aren't about working at the concession stand, or even about Twinkies. Most of the time they're about Ashley. I dream about how after the abortion, her parents moved her out of Nebraska and away from me. But Ashley still loved me, and would sneak out of the house and drive 500 miles through the night just to see me for a couple of hours before having to turn around and drive back. "What are you doing, honey?" I would ask her, sleepy-eyed, as she stared at me from the foot of my bed.

"I missed you," she would whisper back. Then she would take my hand and squeeze it three times. *I. Love. You.* I would squeeze back twice. *How. Much?* Then she would squeeze with both of her hands as hard as she could. *To. The. Sky!!!* That was our thing.

When I wake up from the dream, she's gone, of course. Though that realization saddens a part of me for a moment, what bothers me more than anything is that I've never dreamt about the baby we abandoned. I feel guilty because in my dreams of Ashley I get to relive those feelings of young, untethered love that we never, despite our most earnest efforts, replicate in our adult years. In some twisted way, I suppose I want to be haunted by dreams of the child whose life I prevented. At least then I would feel like I had paid some small penance for the only action in my life that I consider sinful.

I don't believe that there is an omnipotent god who punishes us for our sins, but I know that each of us has a personal conscience that tells us when we've done something wrong. Sometimes all it takes to quiet your conscience is to admit that white lie you've told, or to confess to your landlord that it was you who left the security door open, which allowed a bum to get into your apartment building and take a dump in the stairwell. I can't speak for everyone, but for me, when that something you've done is irreversible and you know you can't take it back, the voice of your conscience never stops whispering in your ear about the evil you've done. It's this unrelenting conscience of mine that keeps me up at night. On rare occasions I'm able to roll over, and with a little head scratching from my wife, fall back asleep. But most nights I get up, turn on the computer, and log-on to visit my old adversary: Facebook.

After all these years I still have one of the wax-coated food wrappers we served the fried Twinkies in, tacked to the cork board by my desk. The text of the Fried Twinkie Manifesto is still perfectly preserved on the crinkled, semi-translucent paper. Sometimes I take it down and nostalgically run my fingers over the oil-stained wrapper as I browse through the mundane details of the virtual lives of my Facebook friends. Though I try to avoid Ashley's page, I sometimes end up there. Mostly I look at the pictures of her and her newborn baby girl. They look perfect together, which has caused me to cry on at least one occasion. And while there's a certain amount of bitterness in the tears, mostly it's just a sincere gratitude I feel toward the universe—or whatever is in charge of these things—for giving her a second chance to be a mom.

By this time it's usually late, and I've got to get up early for work the next morning. I stare at my blank Facebook status, searching for some way to organize my thoughts so the friends with whom I share this virtual reality can begin to understand these feelings I've lugged around for so many years. I desperately need them to know that I'm more than just an acid-taking Twinkie fucker. But my cursor just blinks back mockingly at me. The things I have felt about Ashley and our lost baby cannot be expressed with words.

So I climb back in bed with my sleeping wife. I hold her close and whisper in her ear how much I love her—how grateful I am for the unconditional love she shows me every day, despite the past I've never quite been able to put behind me. Then I surrender to the darkness and fall asleep. In my dreams she and I stand on a high cliff overlooking the ocean. Behind us is an endless stack of computers and individually-wrapped Twinkies, which we hurl, one by one, into the sea below. We yell triumphantly as the hard-drives bubble and then slowly slip below the water's choppy surface. Then I take her in my arms and commandingly embrace her as if we were in an old military poster. And, if only in this dream world, I experience again what it felt like to be whole, before the ghosts of regret chiseled a home for themselves out of the most delicate parts of my heart.

About The Author

Ryan Moehring was born in Nampa, Idaho and raised in Omaha, Nebraska. (He's still not sure what he did to piss off his parents.) Ryan attended Beals Elementary School in Omaha, where, as a result of his unfashionable mullet and husky physique, he was indiscriminately pummeled during recess by white and black kids alike. As a result, to this day he is terrified of playground gravel—won't go near the stuff.

He currently lives in Colorado with his wife and dogs, where he earned his master's degree from Denver University's Sturm College of Law. The Fried Twinkie Manifesto is his first book.